THE MACMILLAN SHAKESPEARE
GENERAL EDITOR: PETER HOLLINDALE,
Senior Lecturer in English and Education,
University of York
ADVISORY EDITOR: PHILIP BROCKBANK,
Professor of English and Director of the
Shakespeare Institute, University of Birmingham

AS YOU LIKE IT

Other titles in the series:

THE MACMILLAN SHAKESPEARE

AS YOU LIKE IT

Edited by

Peter Hollindale

Macmillan Education

First edition 1974
Reprinted 1977, 1982, 1983, 1985 (twice)

Published by
MACMILLAN EDUCATION LTD
Houndmills, Basingstoke, Hampshire RG21 2XS
and London
Companies and representatives
throughout the world

Printed in Hong Kong

ISBN 0-333-14938-6

CONTENTS

INTRODUCTION

J. Dover Wilson gave the title *Shakespeare's Happy Comedies* to his book about the group of plays which includes *As You Like It*. Of all these plays, this is the one which could most unreservedly be described as 'happy', and it is also perhaps the simplest. In most Shakespearean comedy, the happiness of youth and romantic fulfilment is modified by shadows of a darker reality. Sometimes there is the lingering presence of a jealous or malignant killjoy, defeated by the events of the play but standing for disturbing human characteristics which have not been destroyed: Shylock in *The Merchant of Venice*, Malvolio in *Twelfth Night*, Don John in *Much Ado About Nothing*. Sometimes the 'romantic' characters themselves reveal capacities for malice which happy endings cannot entirely erase: the quartet of lovers in *A Midsummer Night's Dream* can be brutal to each other, and Claudio's deliberately public attack on Hero in *Much Ado About Nothing* is too mercilessly violent for us to forget when later they are reconciled. And the romantic world of happy comedy, flawed as it often is by discordant cruelty, is also habitually darkened by suggestions of mortality, and hints of a colder world, a world of the wind and the rain, in which youthful love cannot hope to survive for ever.

As You Like It is unusually free of these darker tones. Certainly it has villains, Duke Frederick and Oliver, but they are firmly placed in the urban world of the court which is abandoned after Act 1, and when they finally reappear – either in person or by report – they have undergone dramatic transformations. Certainly romantic feelings are not allowed to flourish unchecked – sentimentality or excess of feeling are repeatedly mocked and ridiculed. But the mockers of love are not driven on by alienated malice; instead their chief impulse is a cheerful and vigorous delight in exposing folly – a folly to which they themselves are subject. The exception to this self-involvement, Jaques, is the most likeable of cynics, and his posture as the sharp-tongued malcontent is redeemed from malice by his obvious delight in the human spectacle he scoffs at.

Nor is *As You Like It* free from suggestions of mortality, which are focused particularly on the character of Adam. The play does not merely present a golden world of youth: the forest world in which romantic attachments multiply and prosper is also a world of cold and hunger, of weariness and intermittent danger, of suffering age. But the privations of exile are, as Duke Senior asserts at the beginning of Act 2, a means to freedom and liberating simplicities, in which men and women can accomplish states of feeling and insight which were not possible in the restricted world of the court.

Such freedoms are, however, holiday freedoms – they cannot last for ever. At the end of the play it is only Jaques who chooses to remain in Arden; the rest return to the everyday world of the court. But in doing so they are not facing up with reluctance to a hard and inescapable reality; they are freely choosing the way of life which is truly theirs, taking with them not only the romantic fulfilment they have won in Arden, but the civilised and courtly qualities which they brought to Arden in the first place, and which have enabled them to turn banishment into liberty.

It is not only in its quality of persistent happiness that *As You Like It* stands a little apart from the other comedies. Its plot is also unusually simple. Instead of the intricate tangles of the other plays, with their massed confusions, uncertainties, misunderstandings and mistaken identities, *As You Like It* depends for its most important effects on a single deception – Rosalind's masquerade as the boy Ganymede. The centrality of this deception points to the other distinctive feature of the play which we need to notice at this stage – the all-important energy and brilliance, the powerful, inclusive personality of Rosalind herself. Of the many delightful heroines of Shakespearean comedy, it is Rosalind who exerts the most decisive, shaping influence on her play.

THE STRUCTURE AND DEVELOPMENT OF THE PLAY

Shakespeare's exposition of the plot in the opening stages of a play is usually skilful and unobtrusive. *As You Like It*, however, opens with a lengthy and cumbersome speech in which Orlando tells Adam, to our great convenience as an audience, essential bits of family history which Adam knows perfectly well already. Later, when Oliver has summoned Charles the wrestler, there is a clumsy, heavy-handed dialogue which tells us all we need to know about events at the court.

These blatantly informative passages have been criticised as maladroit. There is some justice in the criticism, although neither is *merely* informative. Orlando's speech is concerned with schooling in the virtues of courtesy and civilisation, and sets inborn qualities against those derived from education. The dialogue between Oliver and Charles introduces the idealised, Arcadian conception of forest life, where young men 'fleet the time carelessly, as they did in the golden world'. Both passages deal with natural and unnatural behaviour in family relationships. These are important themes in the play, and they are carefully integrated with the exposition of basic situations so that we are aware of them from the outset.

Nevertheless these tightly-packed preliminary exchanges do illustrate a general point concerning the play's structure. The business of the play – the fundamental conflicts on which it depends – is conducted almost entirely in Act 1. By the end of it Orlando has survived one murderous plot by Oliver, and needs only Adam's report of a second (Act 2, scene 3) to despatch him to the sanctuary of Arden; the first stage of his exile is in effect accomplished when he incurs Duke Frederick's displeasure. Division in one family has been matched by division in another – Rosalind has been denounced and banished by her uncle, and she too is bound for Arden. Irrational malice, the prerogative and seeming

3

norm of those who wield power in the urban world, has twice evicted virtue from its presence.

During this Act we see not only the rancorous and destructive impulses of Oliver and Duke Frederick, but the central positive emotions of the play – the love-at-first-sight of Orlando and Rosalind. The hectic and violent action, both physical and emotional, which we see in this Act is a correct indication of the present corrupt and irrational nature of court society: not only does it give initial pace and impetus to the plot, but it contrasts sharply with the contemplative sanity and leisurely ceremonial existence of the banished Duke in Arden. If Shakespeare is indeed anxious to despatch essential business quickly and get to Arden as soon as possible – which has often been suggested – then it is also true that his method of doing so provides a whole series of meaningful contrasts with the pastoral world that we encounter in the forest.

The crowded activity of Act 1 discharges a further essential function. Since Rosalind is destined to be so dominant a heroine, and one with whom the audience is in complicity through its knowledge of her disguise, there is a risk that Orlando's romantic sufferings will by contrast appear unmanly and foolish. To avoid this it is essential to give a strong first impression of his masculine vigour and toughness. His wrestling bout with Charles establishes this beyond doubt in a memorable 'set-piece' of physical action. It also provides a focal point for the range of feelings he arouses: it frustrates Oliver's malice and indirectly stirs Duke Frederick's, it prompts Celia's admiration and causes Rosalind to fall in love. This event in particular gives focus and definition to an overcrowded phase of the action, and creates in the audience an attitude to Orlando which can be utilised in later scenes.

From the beginning of Act 2 the violence of the opening subsides into a spacious and leisured exploration of the play's essential themes. In Act 2 it is the pastoral life of the forest which takes pride of place. It is given memorable expression in the opening speech by Duke Senior, who prefers the mere physical hardships of banishment to the moral privations of life at court, which is characterised by envy, hypocrisy – and ingratitude. It is characteristic of *As You Like It* that this idealising tendency is subjected to criticism. Jaques criticises it, notably in his parody of 'Under the greenwood tree', and we also see two sets of hungry and exhausted refugees arriving, and are thus deterred from sentimentalising physical want. On the other hand, the ideal is effectively restated both by Amiens' two songs and by the generosity of feeling which pervades the Act, notably in the courteous hospitality of both Corin and the Duke. The privations of forest life are real, but that is not to say that its attractions are illusory.

If Act 2 is chiefly preoccupied with the ideal simplicities of pastoral life, in Act 3 we are principally concerned with romantic love. Once again we have conflicting views, and a series of episodes which throw light on each other, not allowing us to accept the romantic ideal naïvely, but not letting us reject it completely, either. After the initial exchange between Touchstone and Corin, we encounter during this Act three pairs of 'lovers'. One of the pairs, Silvius and Phebe, are a conventional shepherd and shepherdess derived directly from the play's immediate source, Lodge's romance *Rosalynde*, and through that from the pastoral tradition of idealised rural life. Silvius is a conventional pining lover, Phebe a conventional scornful mistress. Their dialogue, unusually for this play, is conducted in verse, and it includes the commonplace romantic exaggerations of pastoral courtship – the lethal nature of unrequited love, and the power of the loved one's scornful eye to inflict grievous wounds. To these exaggerations of the love-stricken Silvius, Phebe replies with an equally exaggerated cruelty of realistic dismissal. If Silvius exaggerates the power of love, Phebe grossly underestimates it. This is a very 'literary', very artificial exchange. The forest of Arden in *As You Like It* is a many-sided world, one side of which is the idealised, shepherd-peopled terrain of pastoral romance, and Silvius and Phebe are exactly the kind of figures we could expect to find there. In its exaggeration and artificiality the love conflict between these two supplies one version of the folly of love.

In violent contrast with it we have Touchstone's courtship of Audrey. Audrey inhabits a very different kind of Arden. She is not an idealised pastoral shepherdess but a real-life peasant goatherd, an ignorant country bumpkin. Her suitor, ironically, is perhaps the one amongst all the exiled court figures who is least able to accommodate himself to the rustic way of life – his cast of mind remains inveterately urban. The spectacle of such as Touchstone wooing a mindless peasant provides another instance of love's absurdity, very different from that of Silvius and Phebe. Not for him the sanctified adoration of an idealised beloved: in his exchange with Jaques (3, iii, 72–93) he is quite explicit about the nature of his motives. 'As the ox hath his bow, sir, the horse his curb, and the falcon her bells, so man hath his desires; and as pigeons bill, so wedlock would be nibbling'.

The 'love' of Touchstone for Audrey is crudely physical. He preserves complete intellectual detachment from it, directs his belittling wit at his loved one, and has no illusions about the likely duration of his attachment. Content as he is that a bad marriage will excuse a good desertion, his realism is in marked contrast with the lover's conventional protestations of eternal faithfulness.

Coming towards the end of the Act, these contrasting relationships not only develop the play's exploration of love, but provide a commentary on the central relationship, that between Rosalind and Orlando. The sudden love that overtook them in Act 1 now begins its strange and entertaining progress in the settled banishment of Arden. We first see Orlando, in Act 3, scene 2, in the conventional role of the stricken and obsessive lover, Silvius-like in his devotion, hanging verses on the trees. Before long these same verses are prompting the mockery of Rosalind, Celia and Touchstone, and love's folly and exaggeration, as expressed by

Orlando, are ridiculed by the untrammelled intelligence of the girls and the jester. But Rosalind's intelligence is untrammelled only briefly. Once she discovers the true identity of the 'poet', her speech and behaviour are determined by her own reciprocal feeling. From this emerges her opportunistic and ingenious plan to use her male disguise as a pretext for luring Orlando into unknowing courtship, under the pretence of curing his afflictions. Once this ruse has worked, her central position as controller and manipulator of the action is firmly established, and it remains so until the end of the play. She is able to express the strength of her own feelings without being known to do so, and to hear Orlando confess in all innocence his love and devotion to her. Yet she is also able, using the advantages of her disguise, to act as the detached and witty analyst of love, of the follies it causes and of the foibles of women. As Ganymede, she can stand outside the action and exploit its comic potential to the full; as Rosalind, she can freely express the depth and sincerity of her own emotional involvement. The audience's knowledge of that involvement redeems her from any suspicions of heartless play-acting, and justifies not only the trick she plays on Orlando but also her interference in the trials of Silvius and Phebe.

Like Touchstone, Rosalind is armed with scepticism and wit, but unlike him her own feeling is not merely physical and her detachment is anything but complete. Like Orlando and Silvius, Rosalind is truly in love, and well-placed to recognise and punish the cruelty of Phebe, but unlike Orlando and Silvius she does not lose her sense of love's absurdity when she experiences its strength. There is nothing cold about her intelligence, nothing naïve about her love. In her own person she combines and balances the characteristics which we see, single and exaggerated, in others, and out of the various follies of love and the various follies of scepticism, she creates a personal order which is central to the play. By the qualities of her character and by her adroit manipulation of events she acquires during this Act a controlling influence over the happenings of the play, the lives of the characters, and the way we in the audience respond to them. When, later in Act 3, we meet opposite extremes of folly in Touchstone and Audrey and in Silvius and Phebe, we can recognise them for what they are.

It will already be clear how the pace of the drama slows down once we have reached Arden after the precipitate events of Act 1. From the beginning of Act 2 the play has a looser, more spacious and flexible design: instead of witnessing the rapid consequences of impetuous malice, we are in a free and leisurely situation where several relationships pursue their courses, running parallel with each other in some respects, contrasting with and illuminating each other. The play's preoccupations with romantic love, and with the qualities of civilisation and pastoral simplicity, are developed in a sequence of scenes which is spatial rather than temporal. In fact time itself has become more a matter for speculative, philosophical contemplation of a half-serious kind, rather than a question of pressing urgency – Touchstone, Jaques and Rosalind all meditate in characteristic ways on the nature of time (2, vii, 20–8; 2, vii, 139–66; and 3, ii, 299–330). Only deprived and impatient lovers become troubled by it.

In Act 4 we again see this characteristic design of the play, which makes measured progress through a series of conversations rather than through an organised sequence of events. Sometimes they advance the plot, such as it is, a little further, though the opening conversation between Rosalind and Jaques does not even do that. More importantly, they deepen the play's examination of its central themes, testing the beliefs and attitudes of one character by exposing them to the censure of another. (It is important that we should find out what Rosalind thinks of Jaques. Her criticism of his attitudes, coupled with her sharp retort to Touchstone in Act 3, scene 2 – 'you'll be rotten ere you be half ripe' – means that both the play's 'fools' have received curt judgement from the heroine.) During this Act we see the promised mock wooing of Ganymede by Orlando, Rosalind sustaining her charade with wit and skill, and in the process contriving both to enjoy herself with critical generalisations about the female nature and to puncture some romantic illusions about love. In this process we see Rosalind as the supreme romantic heroine of comedy, blending levity and seriousness, truth of intellect and truth of feeling.

Yet our sense of space and amplitude in the drama is partly an illusion, resulting from the deft stagecraft with which Shakespeare explores a many-sided reality. In fact this is only Rosalind's second meeting with Orlando in Arden, and the only occasion when the mock wooing is given full play. *As You Like It* may lack intricacy in its plot, but it does not lack intricacy of human relationships. It is a skilfully managed series of confrontations which gives us a many-sided view of people in the condition of love, seen through each other's eyes, and hence a multiple view of love itself.

The meeting of Rosalind and Silvius (Act 4, scene 3) is an example of this. Like the Rosalind – Silvius – Phebe confrontation of Act 3, it relies for its effect on our recent testimony of Rosalind's own depth of love: otherwise her earthy abuse of the absent Phebe, and her teasing of Silvius about the contents of Phebe's letter, might appear gratuitously harsh. But knowing as we do about Rosalind's own dilemma of concealed love, we can instead admire the resilience that she can bring to the task of engineering true and appropriate affections in others.

The brief connecting scene (Act 4, scene 2), when we see Jaques with the hunters, is a more straightforward instance of Shakespeare's dramatic economy. Technically it marks the passage of time while Rosalind is waiting for Orlando's return. But it is not left with so perfunctory a purpose. Instead it reminds us of Duke Senior, who will shortly re-enter the action; it presents in concrete form the simple self-sufficiency which has earlier been advertised as a virtue of pastoral life; and it furnishes the necessary business of hunting with overtones of ceremony and celebration – a public and festive ritual which contrasts with the private sententious moralising that surrounded hunting earlier (2, i, 21–8). Jaques, we should note, participates in both.

With the entrance of Oliver (4, iii, 76) the momentum quickens again as the play moves towards a conclusion. The events that Oliver describes take place off-stage, of course, as do other important events between this and the end of the play; there is none of the visible explosive action of Act 1. Indeed, the very leisureliness and casual development of the action is itself material for comedy as Oliver gives, to Rosalind's intense nervous frustration, his sedate blow-by-blow account of Orlando's recent dangers. But at least there *are* events, and Rosalind's feminine reaction is another of the play's constant reminders that she is after all a woman, and cannot keep up her masculine disguise indefinitely.

In Act 5 the complications issuing from Rosalind's deception are at last resolved, and the Act is a celebration of fulfilled love. There is a seamy side, and we are reminded of it at the start, in Touchstone's ruthless employment of his court wit to warn off the foolish peasant William, but the clown's parody of elaborate courtly language is funny enough to leave the point unstressed. News of the impetuous love affair between Oliver and Celia (putting them on an exactly equal footing with Orlando and Rosalind) cancels Orlando's delight in mere pretences, and so prompts Rosalind to organise the final revelation. The melancholy chant of pious lovers, which concludes Act 5, scene 2, (lines 84–109) is undermined by Rosalind's truthful but seemingly mocking contributions, and finally drives her to impatience: 'Pray you, no more of this: 'tis like the howling of Irish wolves against the moon'. In the series of promises which follows, (5, ii, 112–23) she shows herself in the role she has enacted so skilfully, as the astute stage-manager of feelings and relationships, including her own.

The beautiful lyric 'It was a lover and his lass' introduces the final section of the play: the revelation of Rosalind's identity, the masque of Hymen, and the final ceremony of fourfold marriage, followed by a ritual celebratory dance which represents the unity and harmony achieved. The forest winter of earlier songs is transformed now into spring, the season of union and fertility, and this fulfilment is anticipated by the gay romantic idealism of the Pages' song.

There are two interruptions in the ceremonial process of Act 5. The first is Touchstone's famous account of the 'quarrel upon the seventh cause'. Like the hunting scene in Act 4, this is a time-filler – it enables Rosalind to change back into women's clothes. Like the earlier scene it has a further purpose: it represents a general awareness among the exiles of the hollow superficial ceremonies of court life, which will shortly reclaim them, and it contrasts that hollowness with the true ceremony in which they are now participating. The second interruption brings Jaques de Boys, with news of Duke Frederick's conversion, and the restoration of all properties and rights among the exiles.

There has been much criticism of the play's ending, which is sometimes held to be hurried, clumsy and dependant on cumbersome apparatus such as the unexpected intrusion of Hymen, and on psychological improbabilities such as the sudden conversions of Oliver and Duke Frederick. Certainly there is little attempt at 'realism' in the final Act. But conversions to goodness are not felt to be implausible, because in this play 'goodness', like happiness, is for once the norm. It is the initial sinfulness of both Oliver and Duke Frederick which is felt to be abnormal – they cannot even explain it to themselves. In the circumstances it is less surprising that the magnetism of goodness should finally draw them back.

The end of the play is a celebration of love and order. It is all the more real because it is not fully idealised: the 'blessing' is delivered by Jaques, who is spurning the court in favour of his own kind of priestly celibacy, and he is fully alive to the marital prospects of Touchstone and Audrey. The ideals of courtesy and love which have permeated the play are neither sentimentalised nor destroyed at the end;

nor do they belong exclusively either to Arden or the court, but to both.

COURT AND COUNTRY

It is clear, then, that the stock contrast between court and country is important in *As You Like It*, even though the scenes which take place at court are almost all confined to Act 1. The relationship between the two is not, however, a matter of opposites and straightforward choice. At first it may appear that this is so. Envy and irrational malice determine people's fates in the court world, and in Amiens' songs in Act 2 they are joined by hypocrisy and ingratitude as customary immoral attributes of court life. Duke Senior's speech at the beginning of Act 2 commends the contrasting simplicities of the countryside, and it seems that the play is indeed idealising pastoral existence.

On the other hand, the end of the play could leave us with the opposite conclusion. Whatever pleasure the Duke and his followers have found in Arden, we note that they are ready enough to resume their former lives when Duke Frederick's unlikely conversion offers them the chance, and the mere 'penalty of Adam', the physical hardships that were earlier so preferable to the moral hardships at court, are recollected by Duke Senior as the 'shrewd days and nights' that the exiles have all 'endured'. Has their philosophical delight in rural simplicities amounted to more than making the best of a bad job?

Our feeling, gradually reinforced by the events of the play and the tone of successive scenes, is surely that it has. Despite the preliminary despair and fatigue of the new fugitives, our first experience of Arden establishes a sense of relaxed freedom and contemplative ease which is prevalent among the Duke and his friends – a capacity to improvise holiday delights out of the burden of necessity. We soon see the newcomers behaving in the same way, giving full sway to romantic passion, as Orlando does, or transforming necessitous disguise into enjoyable and prosperous deceptions, as do Rosalind and Celia. Meditative philosophy, acute social observation and intellectual wit, romantic love – all can flourish in Arden with peculiar spaciousness, uncluttered by urban conventionality.

On the other hand, these qualities are all imported from the court, and it is only the behaviour of particular régimes which has put them into exile. The qualities which prosper so happily in the country are not country qualities. It is not that the exiles adapt themselves to rural customs; instead they introduce their own customs and adapt them to the country. In Duke Senior's forest existence we repeatedly see modified customs of the civilised court: music, festive ritual, respect for rank and place, the 'banquet', courteous speech and behaviour, hospitality and gentleness. Later, the mock wooing of Rosalind by Orlando is also governed by civilised courtesies of speech and behaviour; Orlando notices these things in Ganymede, who is compelled to explain them away (3, ii, 331–42). What we see in the play is not a rejection of one life and the choice of another, but an inventive, and indeed a humanly creative, compromise between the two.

If, then, the play does not present a naïve endorsement of pastoral existence, neither does it permit a naïve condemnation of the court. We noticed earlier that the envious malignancy of Oliver and Duke Frederick is depicted as an aberration, an irrational impulse which neither can explain. This in itself suggests that their behaviour should not be seen as typical. The impression is confirmed by our experience of other individuals – of Celia's unwavering loyalty to Rosalind, and Adam's to Orlando, and of le Beau, who despite his affectations gives Orlando a friendly, well-intentioned warning (1, ii, 258–64) and goes on to express other views indicative of sound judgement and sane values. It is confirmed, too, by everything we hear of Sir Rowland de Boys, who is widely remembered with affection; and by the public love and praise which Orlando and Rosalind both arouse (1, i, 164–8 and 1, ii, 274–8). Everything suggests

that the true values of the court are those which we see sur-
viving, in holiday freedom, amongst the banished courtiers
in Arden.

FOOLS IN THE FOREST

Ironically, the greatest compromises with life in Arden are
made by the two characters who most zealously preserve
their intellectual detachment – Touchstone and Jaques.
They are the ones who are least inclined to romanticise the
pleasures of abandoning the court. Touchstone's reaction
to arrival in the forest is, 'Ay, now am I in Arden, the more
fool I. When I was at home I was in a better place, but
travellers must be content', while it is Jaques who thus
parodies Amiens' idealising 'Under the greenwood tree':

> If it do come to pass
> That any man turn ass,
> Leaving his wealth and ease
> A stubborn will to please:
> Ducdame, ducdame, ducdame,
> Here shall he see
> Gross fools as he,
> An if he will come to me.

Yet Touchstone, the mocker of country simplicities, ends
up married to the bumpkin Audrey after a courtship which
burlesques the romantic convention, while Jaques, alone of
all the courtiers who fled with Duke Senior, elects to stay in
the forest when he no longer needs to.

Jaques' delight when he first meets Touchstone – 'A fool,
a fool, I met a fool i' th' forest' (2, vii, 12) – is sustained
throughout the play, and combined with envy of the fool's
licence to utter satiric wit. It announces from the first the
strong links between the two. They are opposites in some
respects: Touchstone is the professional 'fool', Jaques the
amateur; Touchstone is merry, while Jaques assumes a
fashionable melancholy. But these are mere variations on
similar fundamental attitudes. Their cultivated intellectual

detachment is not proof against physical appetites – Touch-stone frankly pursues Audrey to gratify his, while Jaques, according to Duke Senior, in the past 'hast been a libertine/ As sensual as the brutish sting itself'. Nevertheless they derive intellectual delight from mocking contemplation of the world and its follies, finding material for ridicule not only in the foolishness of others, but in their ostensible wisdom: it is Touchstone's satiric moralising on the subject of time which first attracts Jaques (2, vii, 18–34), while Jaques' famous 'seven ages of man' speech (2, vii, 139–66) is also in part a jest at the expense of moralising tendencies. This speech, which is often taken out of context and treated as Shakespeare's sober judgement on the human life-cycle, is really an ingenious elaboration on a moralising sentiment of Duke Senior's. It is the Duke who has drawn the trite comparison between the world and the theatre, prompted by Orlando's description of the suffering Adam:

> This wide and universal theatre
> Presents more woeful pageants than the scene
> Wherein we play in . . . (2, vii, 137–9)

and Jaques develops the idea to the point of absurdity, in a protracted mockery of philosophical caricature. Jaques en-joys his moralising, but part of his enjoyment lies in making fun of it.

In sharing the amusement of moralising – half self-indulgence and half parody – Touchstone and Jaques show their similar dispositions, which resemble each other in spite of their apparent differences. They are the characters who expose the limitations of pastoralism and romantic love, and ridicule the excesses of each. They do not undermine the genuine values which are inherent in these ideals, but their function in the play is to keep them in check. It is wrong to see either as a 'chorus', or a mouth-piece for Shakespeare's own opinions, but on occasions they do seem to speak on behalf of the audience, voicing reservations that an audience might be inclined to make.

The fool's licence to speak, freely expressing his detached, observant intelligence, always runs the risk of sourness when it is misdirected. Here there is perhaps a difference between Touchstone and Jaques. Touchstone's sophisticated courtly wit is sometimes aimed at the native inhabitants of Arden, who for one reason or another are not equipped to withstand it. Jaques, however, habitually directs his criticism at those who deserve it, not least at Touchstone himself. He may be a cynic, and he may be a bit too free with his general censure, but he is also shrewd and wise. It is quite appropriate that he should be the one to 'give away' the Duke and the lovers in a final round of benevolence (5, iv, 186–92), because benevolence has always lain beneath his affected misanthropy. It is also appropriate that his general good wishes should pick out Touchstone's marriage from the others, recognising its inferior nature: in doing so he finally acknowledges the true virtues of romantic love.

HAST ANY PHILOSOPHY?

If it is chiefly Jaques who criticises the tendency of exiled courtiers to idealise the pastoral life, it is chiefly Touchstone who aims his shafts at the country-dwellers themselves. Sometimes his behaviour in itself constitutes a parody: his carnal relationship with Audrey is in comic contrast with Silvius' wooing of Phebe. Sometimes he employs his wit and verbal extravagance at the expense of simpletons – both Audrey and her rejected suitor William receive their share of it. In the view of some critics, Touchstone's encounter with Corin (3, ii, 11–85) is another such instance, with the simple countryman coming off worst.

At first sight this appears to be so. Equipped now with experience of both court and country, Touchstone enlarges on the comparison with a series of paradoxes. How does he like the shepherd's life?

Truly, shepherd, in respect of itself, it is a good life, but in respect that it is a shepherd's life, it is naught. In

respect that it is solitary, I like it very well; but in respect
that it is private, it is a very vile life. Now in respect it is
in the fields, it pleaseth me well; but in respect it is not in
the court, it is tedious. (3, ii, 13–18)

This is simply a verbally adroit way of saying that it all
depends on your point of view, but it is plainly intended to
bamboozle Corin with a string of seemingly irreconcilable
opposites.

When Touchstone ends by asking Corin 'Hast any philosophy in thee, shepherd?', he is living in hope of some mockable reply, and he appears to get it:

No more but that I know the more one sickens, the
worse at ease he is, and that he that wants money, means,
and content is without three good friends; that the property of rain is to wet and fire to burn; that good pasture
makes fat sheep; and that a great cause of the night is lack
of the sun . . . (3, ii, 23–8)

These lines are sometimes read as a succession of simple-
minded truths, in which Corin tries to match Touchstone at
his own game and comically fails. The opposite, surely, is
true: by these solemn statements of the obvious Corin is
poking fun at Touchstone's verbal ingenuities, and is showing that he has noticed the emptiness behind the wit. Of
course Corin cannot go on winning when the game is played
with words, which are Touchstone's bread and butter, but
he puts up a good resistance, and in the process utters some
sound country sense in language that would not disgrace a
courtier. The climax of his effort is the lovely speech in
which he declares his pastoral philosophy:

Sir, I am a true labourer: I earn that I eat, get that I
wear, owe no man hate, envy no man's happiness, glad of
other men's good, content with my harm; and the greatest
of my pride is to see my ewes graze and my lambs suck.
(3, ii, 73–7)

Touchstone's quick-witted repartee is no answer to that. There is much 'philosophy' brought to Arden from the court – some of it sensible and some not. If we ask, with Touchstone, whether the countryside has any philosophy of its own to offer in return, the answer must be that it has, and Corin is its spokesman. His importance in the design of the play should not be overlooked. His language has a courtly balance, eloquence and dignity, and his behaviour also matches with simple impressiveness the best values of courtly life: it is Corin's courteous hospitality to Rosalind and Celia which is the counterpart of Duke Senior's to Orlando and Adam. To these qualities we can add the note which is distinctively his own: the note of rural contentment and humility which he expresses in reply to Touchstone, a humility which is wholly consistent with a legitimate and admirable pride, and which expresses a true philosophy.

STYLE AND LANGUAGE

The exchange between Touchstone and Corin, quoted above, is a convenient example of the play's extraordinary stylistic virtuosity. Touchstone's speech is a highly organised, formally structured piece of verbal wit, and characteristically so, but what deserves to be noticed is the deftly modulated formality of Corin's initial reply, which abandons the balanced antitheses of Touchstone and yet imitates them closely enough to indicate the shrewdness of his own response, and his verbal skill in expressing it. From this his prose can modulate further to the seemingly total simplicity of his countryman's philosophy, which in fact derives much of its impressiveness from its extended closing cadence, contrasting with the series of simple clauses that precedes it. The effect is to give linguistic form and shape to the deep-rooted and fundamental conviction of Corin's creed.

Controlled formality of language can ennoble a character like Corin. Apparent lack of control can be the medium of psychological truthfulness and comic perspective for Rosalind, when she hears of Celia's encounter with Orlando:

Alas the day, what shall I do with my doublet and hose? What did he when thou sawest him? What said he? How looked he? Wherein went he? What makes he here? Did he ask for me? Where remains he? How parted he with thee? And when shalt thou see him again? Answer me in one word. (3, ii, 219–24)

The lack of control is *only* apparent, of course: the series of breathless questions is accumulated for comic effect – the verbal comedy of that impossible final sentence. Yet the speech is also a perfectly convincing expression of Rosalind's womanly impatience, even to the extent of the dismayed opening question in which she instinctively thinks of her appearance. The particular magic of Rosalind, of course, is that we feel her apparently spontaneous bursts of emotional rhetoric to be partly deliberate, self-knowing and self-mocking – she can experience feeling deeply, and exaggerate it playfully, at one and the same moment. Hence her language is partly a game, and its vivacity is a sign of her playfulness, but it is also the expression of profound emotion. The games and exaggerations are often a way of exhibiting her womanly nature to Celia, with whom it is a constant relief to share the secret, and Celia responds with a jocular everyday practicality which supplies what Rosalind needs from her confidante:

ROSALIND . . . I cannot be out of the sight of Orlando.
I'll go find a shadow and sigh till he come.
CELIA And I'll sleep. (4. i. 215–18)

As in other respects, Rosalind in her language represents a general truth about *As You Like It*. Her speeches are varied and versatile, using a multitude of tones and structures. The play as a whole displays comparable range and elasticity. This is perhaps most easily seen in the verse. Orlando's poetic speeches can encompass the solemn moralising sententiousness of his speech in praise of Adam's loyalty (2, iii, 56–68), the formally and repetitively structured speech of appeal to Duke Senior (2, vii, 106–19) and the trite, mooning romanticism of his paper-hanging oration (3, ii, 1–10). His preposterous love-poems are parodied with extreme indecency by Touchstone, without the need to change the verse-form in the slightest. Not only does the play employ a wide range of verse-forms but, as in this instance, identical forms are skilfully adapted to produce sharp comic contrasts and switches of mood.

However, *As You Like It* is written primarily, and to an unusual extent, in prose – a form more generally suitable than verse for its comic-romantic vein. In general it switches to verse only at its most solemn or most artificial moments. Its prose, like its verse, has extraordinary suppleness, energy and variation, and the examples we looked at above, from Touchstone and Corin, and from Rosalind and Celia, are characteristic of the play's general linguistic strategy, in which formal structures such as antithesis, rhetorical questioning and repetitions are used to achieve a wide range of effects, including a rich colloquial, conversational freedom.

The imagery of *As You Like It* does not fall into the meaningful patterns, or 'clusters', that critics in recent years have recognised elsewhere in Shakespeare, particularly in the major tragedies. But Caroline Spurgeon, that indefatigable collector of images, has usefully pointed out that the play contains numerous references to animals and to other elements of country life, and that the rural atmosphere of the forest depends on these rather than on actual descriptions or evocations of the landscape. One should add that the animal references range from the completely domesticated (sheep and goats) to the dangerously wild (snakes and lions). This range reflects the double nature of Arden in the play: it is both an orderly, gracious pastoral scene, and a 'desert' or wilderness in which travellers may face extreme danger and privation.

DATE AND SOURCE

As You Like It was entered in the Stationers' Register – a means of establishing ownership and copyright – in August

1600. It is not included in Francis Meres' inventory of Shakespeare's plays in *Palladis Tamia* (1598), so the date of composition is set some time in these two years. Celia's reference (Act 1, scene 2) to the time when 'the little wit that fools have was silenced', is often taken as a topical reference to an order of 1599 banning satiric writing, and if this is so, the likeliest dates for *As You Like It* are late 1599 or early 1600.

The source of *As You Like It* is a pastoral romance by Thomas Lodge, *Rosalynde or Euphues' Golden Treasury*, published in 1590, and much of the plot, characterisation and detailed situation is derived from this work. One example will suffice to indicate the kind of debt Shakespeare owes: compare Orlando's opening speech concerning Oliver's treatment of himself and his brother (Act 1, scene 1, 1–25) with this passage from *Rosalynde*, in which Saladyne, (the equivalent of Oliver) meditates his intentions first for Rosader (Orlando) and then Fernandyne (Jaques de Boys):

> Let him know little, so shall he not be able to execute much; suppress his wits with a base estate, and though he be a gentleman by nature, yet form him anew, and make him a peasant by nurture; so shalt thou keep him as a slave, and reign thyself sole lord over all thy father's possessions. As for Fernandyne, thy middle brother, he is a scholar and hath no mind but on Aristotle; let him read on Galen while thou riflest with gold, and pore on his book till thou dost purchase lands. Wit is great wealth; if he have learning it is enough: and so let all rest.

Shakespeare rearranged the plot he found in *Rosalynde*, removing most of its violence and establishing closer relationships between some of the characters. By far the most important alteration he made was to introduce Touchstone and Jaques, who do not appear in *Rosalynde* and who are essential to the effect of *As You Like It*.

A NOTE ON THE TEXT

As You Like It was first printed in the First Folio of Shakespeare's plays (1623). It is among the least problematical of all Shakespearean texts and may well have been based on a copy used in the theatre and carefully prepared for printing: its clear division into acts and scenes suggests that this is so. This edition adheres closely to the Folio text, but obvious errors have been corrected and a number of widely accepted emendations included. One of these deserves special comment. At 2, i, 5 the Folio text of Duke Senior's speech reads: 'Here feel we *not* the penalty of Adam'. Theobald's emendation, 'Here feel we *but* the penalty of Adam', has been accepted by most subsequent editors, but recent editions have tended to restore the Folio reading, offering some ingenious explanations which support it without altering the essential meaning of the speech. Nevertheless the case for Theobald's reading, which simplifies the grammatical structure and makes plain a contrast which is intrinsic to the play, remains strong and convincing, and I have accordingly retained it.

AS YOU LIKE IT

THE CHARACTERS

DUKE SENIOR, banished in the Forest of Arden

JAQUES
AMIENS } noblemen attending on Duke Senior

DUKE FREDERICK, brother of Duke Senior, usurper of the
dukedom

LE BEAU, a courtier attending on Duke Frederick

CHARLES, a wrestler

OLIVER
JAQUES } sons of Sir Rowland de Boys
ORLANDO

ADAM
DENNIS } servants of Oliver

TOUCHSTONE, a clown

SIR OLIVER MARTEXT, a country vicar

CORIN
SILVIUS } shepherds

WILLIAM, a country yokel, in love with Audrey

ROSALIND, daughter of Duke Senior, later disguised as
Ganymede

CELIA, daughter of Duke Frederick, later disguised as Aliena

PHEBE, a shepherdess

AUDREY, a country wench

A person representing HYMEN

Lords, pages and attendants

ACT ONE, scene 1

The opening scene's function is partly informative: it gives necessary background information about the causes of the situation we see. It also introduces themes which concern the play as a whole – inborn virtue, which hostile circumstances cannot destroy (Orlando) and envy of other men's virtues (Oliver).

[2] by will   *in (my father's) will*
> but poor a thousand   *merely a thousand*

[3–4] charged . . . breed me   *my brother was instructed to educate me, as a condition of receiving our father's blessing*

[6] goldenly . . . profit   *approvingly of his progress*

[8] properly   *truly*
> stays   *detains*
> unkept   *uneducated; unsupported*

[11] fair with   *healthy and vigorous because of*

[12] taught . . . manage   *taught their paces; trained*

[13] riders   *horse-trainers*
> dearly   *expensively*

[15] bound   *indebted*

[16–17] Besides . . . gives me   *Besides giving me such a plentiful supply of nothing*

[17] something . . . gave me   *the personal qualities I inherited at birth*
> his countenance   *the way of life he allows me*

[19] hinds   *servants*
> bars me   *deprives me of*

[19–21] as much as . . . education   *as far as he is able, undermines my noble birth by my poor education*

[28] shake me up   *castigate me*

ACT ONE

Scene 1. *Enter* ORLANDO *and* ADAM

ORLANDO As I remember, Adam, it was upon this fashion bequeathed me by will but poor a thousand crowns, and, as thou say'st, charged my brother on his blessing to breed me well; and there begins my sadness. My brother Jaques he keeps at school, and report speaks goldenly of his profit. For my part, he keeps me rustically at home or, to speak more properly, stays me here at home, unkept; for call you that 'keeping' for a gentleman of my birth that differs not from the stalling of an ox? His horses are 10 bred better, for, besides that they are fair with their feeding, they are taught their manage, and to that end riders dearly hired; but I, his brother, gain nothing under him but growth, for the which his animals on his dunghills are as much bound to him as I. Besides this nothing that he so plentifully gives me, the something that nature gave me his countenance seems to take from me. He lets me feed with his hinds, bars me the place of a brother, and, as much as in him lies, mines my gentility with my 20 education. This is it, Adam, that grieves me; and the spirit of my father, which I think is within me, begins to mutiny against this servitude. I will no longer endure it, though yet I know no wise remedy how to avoid it.

Enter OLIVER

ADAM Yonder comes my master, your brother.

ORLANDO Go apart, Adam, and thou shalt hear how he will shake me up.

ADAM *stands apart*

[29] what make you . . .? *what are you doing . . .? Orlando replies with a pun, taking 'make' to mean 'construct'.*

[32] Marry *By the Virgin Mary*

[35-6] be naught awhile *be off and don't trouble me*

[37-8] Shall I . . . spent *Orlando refers to the parable of the Prodigal Son (see Luke 15. 11 and following) and asks whether he has incurred his poverty by previous wastefulness.*

[40] where you are *in whose company you are. Orlando pretends to take 'where' literally.*

[43] him I am before *i.e. Oliver*

[44-5] gentle . . . blood *manner appropriate for a well-born brother*

[46] courtesy *established custom (of giving precedence to the first-born son)*

allows *acknowledges*

[48] blood *breeding*

[50-1] coming . . . reverence *as the elder you have inherited a greater share of the respect due to him*

[52] What, boy! *'Boy' is insulting. Oliver is angered both by Orlando's repeated reference to the traditions of courtesy, and by his subdued insolence of tone.*

[54] young in this *inexperienced in fighting. Orlando turns Oliver's seniority against him.*

[55] villain *rascal. Orlando takes up the word's other meaning of 'low-born person'.*

[61-2] railed on thyself *attacked yourself (in slandering Orlando's parentage, which he shares)*

OLIVER   Now, sir, what make you here?

ORLANDO   Nothing. I am not taught to make anything.   30

OLIVER   What mar you then, sir?

ORLANDO   Marry, sir, I am helping you to mar that
which God made, a poor unworthy brother of yours,
with idleness.

OLIVER   Marry, sir, be better employed, and be naught
awhile.

ORLANDO   Shall I keep your hogs and eat husks with
them? What prodigal portion have I spent that I
should come to such penury?

OLIVER   Know you where you are, sir?   40

ORLANDO   O, sir, very well. Here in your orchard.

OLIVER   Know you before whom, sir?

ORLANDO   Ay, better than him I am before knows me:
I know you are my eldest brother, and in the gentle
condition of blood you should so know me. The
courtesy of nations allows you my better, in that you
are the first born, but the same tradition takes not
away my blood were there twenty brothers betwixt
us. I have as much of my father in me as you, albeit
I confess your coming before me is nearer to his   50
reverence.

OLIVER   What, boy!

Strikes him

ORLANDO   Come, come, elder brother, you are too
young in this.

Seizes him

OLIVER   Wilt thou lay hands on me, villain?

ORLANDO   I am no villain. I am the youngest son of
Sir Rowland de Boys; he was my father, and he is
thrice a villain that says such a father begot villains.
Wert thou not my brother, I would not take this
hand from thy throat till this other had pulled out   60
thy tongue for saying so. Thou hast railed on thyself.

27

[70] qualities *behaviour and accomplishments*

[72] exercises . . . become *occupations which befit*
[73] allottery *share of our inheritance*
[78] will *(i) inheritance from your father's will; (ii) wishes*

[79] becomes *befits*

[83–4] 'God . . . master' *A clear portrait of the dead Sir Rowland emerges: he was peaceable, spirited, generous to servants. Compare with Oliver and Orlando.*

[85] grow upon me *grow up and become troublesome to me*
[86] physic . . . rankness *dose you with something to cure your over-growth. Overgrown weeds were commonly described as 'rank'.*

[91] So please you *If it pleases you*
[93–4] 'Twill . . . way *Oliver is already plotting a way to dispose of Orlando.*

Enter CHARLES *The arrival of Charles from the court introduces the second stage of exposition in the scene. We are quickly and concisely informed of the changes which have overtaken the dukedom, and this permits a brisk introduction to Scene 2.*

ADAM [*comes forward*]   Sweet masters, be patient. For
your father's remembrance, be at accord.

OLIVER   Let me go, I say.

ORLANDO   I will not till I please. You shall hear me.
My father charged you in his will to give me good
education. You have trained me like a peasant,
obscuring and hiding from me all gentlemanlike
qualities. The spirit of my father grows strong in   70
me, and I will no longer endure it. Therefore allow
me such exercises as may become a gentleman, or
give me the poor allottery my father left me by
testament; with that I will go buy my fortunes.

OLIVER   And what wilt thou do, beg when that is
spent? Well, sir, get you in. I will not long be
troubled with you. You shall have some part of your
will. I pray you leave me.

ORLANDO   I will no further offend you than becomes
me for my good.   80

OLIVER   Get you with him, you old dog.

ADAM   Is 'old dog' my reward? Most true, I have lost
my teeth in your service. God be with my old
master; he would not have spoke such a word.

[*Exeunt* ORLANDO *and* ADAM

OLIVER   Is it even so? Begin you to grow upon me?
I will physic your rankness and yet give no thousand
crowns neither. Holla, Dennis!

Enter DENNIS

DENNIS   Calls your worship?

OLIVER   Was not Charles, the Duke's wrestler, here to
speak with me?   90

DENNIS   So please you, he is here at the door and
importunes access to you.

OLIVER   Call him in. [*Exit* DENNIS] 'Twill be a good
way – and tomorrow the wrestling is.

Enter CHARLES

[103] good leave *willing permission*

[110] to stay *if compelled to stay*

[118–19] fleet . . . world *make the time pass quickly, free from cares, as they did in the Golden Age*

[122] Marry *By the Virgin Mary*

[124–5] disposition *inclination*

[126] fall *bout of wrestling*
    for my credit *to defend my reputation*
[127] shall *must*
[129] tender *undeveloped and inexperienced*
    for your love *out of regard for you*
    foil *defeat; overthrow*

CHARLES Good morrow to your worship.

OLIVER Good Monsieur Charles, what's the new news at the new court?

CHARLES There's no news at the court, sir, but the old news. That is, the old Duke is banished by his younger brother the new Duke, and three or four 100 loving lords have put themselves into voluntary exile with him, whose lands and revenues enrich the new Duke; therefore he gives them good leave to wander.

OLIVER Can you tell if Rosalind, the Duke's daughter, be banished with her father?

CHARLES O, no; for the Duke's daughter, her cousin, so loves her, being ever from their cradles bred together, that she would have followed her exile, or have died to stay behind her. She is at the court, 110 and no less beloved of her uncle than his own daughter, and never two ladies loved as they do.

OLIVER Where will the old Duke live?

CHARLES They say he is already in the Forest of Arden, and a many merry men with him; and there they live like the old Robin Hood of England. They say many young gentlemen flock to him every day, and fleet the time carelessly as they did in the golden world.

OLIVER What, you wrestle tomorrow before the new 120 Duke?

CHARLES Marry, do I sir; and I came to acquaint you with a matter. I am given, sir, secretly to understand that your younger brother, Orlando, hath a disposition to come in disguised against me to try a fall. Tomorrow, sir, I wrestle for my credit, and he that escapes me without some broken limb shall acquit him well. Your brother is but young and tender, and for your love I would be loath to foil him, as I must for my own honour if he come in. 130 Therefore, out of my love to you, I came hither to

[132] withal *with it*

[132–3] stay . . . intendment *prevent him from carrying out his intentions*

[133] brook *endure*

[137] kindly requite *generously return*

[138] herein *in this matter*

[139] underhand *indirect, inconspicuous. This word did not as yet imply automatically that deception was being practised.*

[142] envious emulator *jealous and malignant rival*

[143] parts *abilities*

[144] natural *by birth. The word 'natural' has ironic undertones, since Oliver's attitude to Orlando is 'unnatural' in a brother. In this part of the speech Oliver is virtually describing himself.*

[146–9] thou wert best . . . poison *and you had better be on your guard, because if you injure him slightly, or if he does not enhance his reputation by defeating you, he will plot to poison you*

[148] practice *plot*

[154] brotherly *with the understatement natural in a brother*
        anatomize *literally 'dissect a corpse' and hence 'describe in full detail'*

[158] payment *just deserts*

[159] go alone *walk without crutches*

[161] stir *provoke, spur on*

[162] gamester *athlete. Oliver speaks scornfully.*

[164] gentle *gentlemanly*

[165] noble device *gentlemanly intentions*

[165–6] of all sorts . . . beloved *loved by all kinds of people as if he cast a spell over them*

[166] in the heart . . . world *taken to their hearts by all people*

[168] misprized *despised*

acquaint you withal, that either you might stay him
from his intendment, or brook such disgrace well as
he shall run into, in that it is a thing of his own
search, and altogether against my will.

OLIVER Charles, I thank thee for thy love to me,
which thou shalt find I will most kindly requite. I
had myself notice of my brother's purpose herein,
and have by underhand means laboured to dissuade
him from it; but he is resolute. I'll tell thee, Charles, 140
it is the stubbornest young fellow of France; full of
ambition, an envious emulator of every man's good
parts, a secret and villainous contriver against me,
his natural brother. Therefore use thy discretion. I
had as lief thou didst break his neck as his finger.
And thou wert best look to't; for if thou dost him
any slight disgrace, or if he do not mightily grace
himself on thee, he will practice against thee by
poison, entrap thee by some treacherous device, and
never leave thee till he hath ta'en thy life by some 150
indirect means or other; for, I assure thee – and
almost with tears I speak it – there is not one so
young and so villainous this day living. I speak but
brotherly of him, but should I anatomize him to
thee as he is, I must blush and weep, and thou must
look pale and wonder.

CHARLES I am heartily glad I came hither to you. If
he come tomorrow, I'll give him his payment. If
ever he go alone again, I'll never wrestle for prize
more. And so God keep your worship.   [Exit 160

OLIVER Farewell, good Charles. Now will I stir this
gamester. I hope I shall see an end of him; for my
soul – yet I know not why – hates nothing more than
he. Yet he's gentle, never schooled and yet learned,
full of noble device, of all sorts enchantingly beloved; and indeed so much in the heart of the world,
and especially of my own people, who best know
him, that I am altogether misprized. But it shall not

[169] clear all *settle all problems*

[170] kindle . . . thither *stir the boy up to attend the wrestling*

ACT ONE, scene 2

In this scene the two main family groups are brought together, with strong hints of the future shape of the romance. The sisterly affection of Rosalind and Celia contrasts sharply with the two pairs of alienated brothers, the two Dukes, and Oliver and Orlando.

[1] coz *literally a shortened form of 'cousin', and hence strictly true of Celia and Rosalind. But the word is often used as a general term of affection.*

[2–3] I show . . . mistress of *I appear merrier than I really am*

[3] would you . . . merrier? *do you wish me to be merrier still? The Folio text reads 'would you yet were merrier' – i.e. 'I wish you were merrier than you are, regardless of my own feelings'.*

[5] learn *teach*

[10] so *provided that*

[11] my love *i.e. 'my love for Rosalind'*

take *accept*

[12–13] righteously tempered *correctly blended*

[15] estate *fortunes*

[16–17] nor none . . . have *and is unlikely to have more children*

[19] perforce *by force*

render *give back to*

[26] Marry *By the Virgin Mary*

withal *with it*

[27–9] nor no further . . . come off again *and do not give any man, even in fun, more love than you can safely and honourably abandon at the cost of nothing more than an innocent blush. This speech is deeply ironical in the light of later events, yet love does remain a sport, even at its most serious.*

[31] housewife Fortune *The goddess Fortune, turning her wheel, is lightly compared to a simple housewife at her spinning-wheel.*

be so long; this wrestler shall clear all. Nothing
remains but that I kindle the boy thither, which 170
now I'll go about.   [*Exit*

Scene 2. *Enter* ROSALIND *and* CELIA

CELIA   I pray thee, Rosalind, sweet my coz, be merry.
ROSALIND   Dear Celia, I show more mirth than I am
  mistress of, and would you yet I were merrier?
  Unless you could teach me to forget a banished
  father, you must not learn me how to remember
  any extraordinary pleasure.
CELIA   Herein I see thou lov'st me not with the full
  weight that I love thee. If my uncle, thy banished
  father, had banished thy uncle, the Duke my father,
  so thou hadst been still with me, I could have taught   10
  my love to take thy father for mine. So wouldst thou,
  if the truth of thy love to me were so righteously
  tempered as mine is to thee.
ROSALIND   Well, I will forget the condition of my
  estate to rejoice in yours.
CELIA   You know my father hath no child but I, nor
  none is like to have; and truly, when he dies, thou
  shalt be his heir: for what he hath taken away from
  thy father perforce, I will render thee again in
  affection. By mine honour, I will, and when I break   20
  that oath, let me turn monster. Therefore, my sweet
  Rose, my dear Rose, be merry.
ROSALIND   From henceforth I will, coz, and devise
  sports. Let me see – what think you of falling in
  love?
CELIA   Marry, I prithee, do, to make sport withal;
  but love no man in good earnest, nor no further in
  sport neither than with safety of a pure blush thou
  mayst in honour come off again.
ROSALIND   What shall be our sport then?   30
CELIA   Let us sit and mock the good housewife Fortune

35

[34] would   *wish*

[35–6] bountiful blind woman   *The goddess Fortune was blind.*

[37] fair   *beautiful*

[38] honest   *chaste*

[39] ill-favouredly   *unattractive*

[40–1] Fortune's office . . . Nature's   *Nature was responsible for inborn gifts such as beauty and intelligence, Fortune for acquired gifts such as riches, which can be both gained and lost.*

   office   *duty*

[45] flout   *mock*

[48] Nature's natural   *a born fool. A 'natural' is a half-wit, whereas a professional fool like Touchstone is witty and clever. Rosalind is therefore poking fun at Touchstone.*

[50] Peradventure   *perhaps*

[52] reason of   *talk intelligently about*

[53] natural . . . whetstone   *fool to sharpen our wits*

[54] dullness   *stupidity*

[55] wit . . . wander you   *a play on the fool's 'wandering wits'*

[59–60] No . . . come for you   *By saying 'no' and 'yes' to Celia's question at one and the same time, Touchstone invites her to question his oath, and so initiates the 'witty' exchange which follows.*

[63] pancakes   *fritters*

[64] naught   *worthless*

[64–5] stand to it   *swear to it*

[66] forsworn   *in breach of his oath*

from her wheel, that her gifts may henceforth be
bestowed equally.

ROSALIND   I would we could do so, for her benefits
are mightly misplaced, and the bountiful blind
woman doth most mistake in her gifts to women.

CELIA   'Tis true, for those that she makes fair, she
scarce makes honest, and those that she makes
honest, she makes very ill-favouredly.

ROSALIND   Nay, now thou goest from Fortune's office   40
to Nature's. Fortune reigns in gifts of the world, not
in the lineaments of Nature.

Enter TOUCHSTONE, *the Clown*

CELIA   No; when Nature hath made a fair creature,
may she not by Fortune fall into the fire? Though
Nature hath given us wit to flout at Fortune, hath
not Fortune sent in this fool to cut off the argument?

ROSALIND   Indeed, there is Fortune too hard for
Nature, when Fortune makes Nature's natural the
cutter-off of Nature's wit.

CELIA   Peradventure this is not Fortune's work   50
neither, but Nature's, who perceiveth our natural
wits too dull to reason of such goddesses and hath
sent this natural for our whetstone. For always the
dullness of the fool is the whetstone of the wits.
How now, wit; whither wander you?

TOUCHSTONE   Mistress, you must come away to your
father.

CELIA   Were you made the messenger?

TOUCHSTONE   No, by mine honour, but I was bid to
come for you.   60

ROSALIND   Where learned you that oath, fool?

TOUCHSTONE   Of a certain knight that swore by his
honour they were good pancakes, and swore by his
honour the mustard was naught. Now I'll stand to
it the pancakes were naught and the mustard was
good, and yet was not the knight forsworn.

37

[74] that that is not   *that which does not exist (i.e. their beards)*

[77] sworn it away   *i.e. by breaking oaths*

[84] taxation   *slander, criticism*

[87] By my troth   *By my faith*
[87–9] since the little wit . . . great show   *This may be a reference to a ruling by the Privy Council in 1599 that some offensive satirical pamphlets should be burned, and no more published.*

[92] put on   *force on*

[95] the more marketable   *more easily sold (because heavier)*

[99] colour   *kind*

CELIA How prove you that in the great heap of your
knowledge?

ROSALIND Ay, marry, now unmuzzle your wisdom.

TOUCHSTONE Stand you both forth now. Stroke your 70
chins, and swear by your beards that I am a knave.

CELIA By our beards – if we had them – thou art.

TOUCHSTONE By my knavery – if I had it – then I were;
but if you swear by that that is not, you are not forsworn; no more was this knight, swearing by his
honour, for he never had any; or if he had, he had
sworn it away before ever he saw those pancakes or
that mustard.

CELIA Prithee, who is't that thou mean'st?

TOUCHSTONE One that old Frederick, your father, 80
loves.

CELIA My father's love is enough to honour him
enough. Speak no more of him; you'll be whipped
for taxation one of these days.

TOUCHSTONE The more pity that fools may not speak
wisely what wise men do foolishly.

CELIA By my troth, thou sayest true, for since the
little wit that fools have was silenced, the little
foolery that wise men have makes a great show.
Here comes Monsieur Le Beau. 90

Enter LE BEAU

ROSALIND With his mouth full of news.

CELIA Which he will put on us as pigeons feed their
young.

ROSALIND Then shall we be news-crammed.

CELIA All the better: we shall be the more marketable.
Bon jour, Monsieur Le Beau, what's the news?

LE BEAU Fair princess, you have lost much good
sport.

CELIA Sport? Of what colour?

LE BEAU What colour, madam? How shall I answer 100
you?

[103] Or as . . . decrees *Touchstone imitates Le Beau's affectations, as Celia and Rosalind have already begun to do. Touchstone's imitation is more exaggerated than theirs, as Celia acknowledges (with approval) in the next line.*

[105] rank *i.e. as a witty fool*

[106] smell *Rosalind puns on 'rank' meaning 'strong-smelling'.*

[107] amaze *bewilder*

[108–9] lost the sight of *missed*

[113] yet to do *still to come*

[115] dead and buried *already over and done with*

[118] proper *handsome*

[120] bills *notices*

[120–1] 'Be it known . . . presents' *the formal opening of a legal proclamation. Rosalind mocks Le Beau's stilted language and puns on resence/presents.*

[124] that *so that*

[127] dole *lamentation*

[138] broken music *broken instruments (?). This is usually explained as 'part music', arranged for performance by different instruments, but this does not make very satisfactory sense in what is clearly a musical analogy with bruised or broken bones.*

ROSALIND   As wit and fortune will.

TOUCHSTONE   Or as the Destinies decrees.

CELIA   Well said; that was laid on with a trowel.

TOUCHSTONE   Nay, if I keep not my rank –

ROSALIND   Thou losest thy old smell.

LE BEAU   You amaze me, ladies. I would have told you of good wrestling, which you have lost the sight of.

ROSALIND   Yet tell us the manner of the wrestling.   110

LE BEAU   I will tell you the beginning; and if it please your ladyships, you may see the end, for the best is yet to do, and here, where you are, they are coming to perform it.

CELIA   Well, the beginning that is dead and buried.

LE BEAU   There comes an old man and his three sons –

CELIA   I could match this beginning with an old tale.

LE BEAU   Three proper young men, of excellent growth and presence.

ROSALIND   With bills on their necks: 'Be it known 120 unto all men by these presents.'

LE BEAU   The eldest of the three wrestled with Charles, the Duke's wrestler; which Charles in a moment threw him and broke three of his ribs, that there is little hope of life in him. So he served the second, and so the third. Yonder they lie, the poor old man, their father, making such pitiful dole over them that all the beholders take his part with weeping.

ROSALIND   Alas!

TOUCHSTONE   But what is the sport, monsieur, that 130 the ladies have lost?

LE BEAU   Why, this that I speak of.

TOUCHSTONE   Thus men may grow wiser every day. It is the first time that ever I heard breaking of ribs was sport for ladies.

CELIA   Or I, I promise thee.

ROSALIND   But is there any else longs to see this broken music in his sides? Is there yet another dotes

41

Flourish *Fanfare*

[147] his own peril . . . forwardness *his danger results from his own foolhardiness*

[150] successfully *like someone who could win*

[155] such odds in the man *so much in Charles' favour*
[156] fain *gladly*

[171–4] if you saw . . . equal enterprise *if you saw and assessed yourself properly, fear of your likely fate would warn you to choose a more equal opponent*

upon rib-breaking? Shall we see this wrestling, cousin? 140

LE BEAU You must, if you stay here, for here is the place appointed for the wrestling, and they are ready to perform it.

CELIA Yonder, sure, they are coming. Let us now stay and see it.

Flourish. Enter DUKE FREDERICK, LORDS, ORLANDO, CHARLES *and* ATTENDANTS

DUKE FREDERICK Come on. Since the youth will not be entreated, his own peril on his forwardness.

ROSALIND Is yonder the man?

LE BEAU Even he, madam.

CELIA Alas, he is too young; yet he looks successfully. 150

DUKE FREDERICK How now, daughter and cousin; are you crept hither to see the wrestling?

ROSALIND Ay, my liege, so please you give us leave.

DUKE FREDERICK You will take little delight in it, I can tell you, there is such odds in the man. In pity of the challenger's youth I would fain dissuade him, but he will not be entreated. Speak to him, ladies; see if you can move him.

CELIA Call him hither, good Monsieur Le Beau.

DUKE FREDERICK Do so. I'll not be by. [*Stands aside* 160

LE BEAU Monsieur the challenger, the princess calls for you.

ORLANDO I attend them with all respect and duty.

ROSALIND Young man, have you challenged Charles the wrestler?

ORLANDO No, fair princess. He is the general challenger; I come but in as others do, to try with him the strength of my youth.

CELIA Young gentleman, your spirits are too bold for your years. You have seen cruel proof of this man's 170 strength; if you saw yourself with your eyes or knew

[177] therefore be misprized *be despised because of this*
    suit *petition*
[179–80] with . . . thoughts *by thinking me ungracious*
[180] wherein *in a matter in which*

[183] wherein *in which*
    foiled *defeated, thrown*
[184] gracious *favoured by Fortune*

[187] Only in the world I . . . *In the world I only . . .*
[188] supplied *occupied*

[193] deceived *mistaken (by having underrated your chances)*

[199] working *ambition (namely, to throw Charles)*

[201] warrant *assure*

[205] come your ways *come on, let's start*
[206] be thy speed *aid you*

yourself with your judgement, the fear of your adventure would counsel you to a more equal enterprise. We pray you for your own sake to embrace your own safety and give over this attempt.

ROSALIND Do, young sir. Your reputation shall not therefore be misprized: we will make it our suit to the Duke that the wrestling might not go forward.

ORLANDO I beseech you, punish me not with your hard thoughts, wherein I confess me much guilty to 180 deny so fair and excellent ladies anything. But let your fair eyes and gentle wishes go with me to my trial; wherein if I be foiled, there is but one shamed that was never gracious; if killed, but one dead that is willing to be so. I shall do my friends no wrong, for I have none to lament me; the world no injury, for in it I have nothing. Only in the world I fill up a place which may be better supplied when I have made it empty.

ROSALIND The little strength that I have, I would it 190 were with you.

CELIA And mine to eke out hers.

ROSALIND Fare you well. Pray heaven I be deceived in you!

CELIA Your heart's desires be with you!

CHARLES Come, where is this young gallant that is so desirous to lie with his mother earth?

ORLANDO Ready, sir; but his will hath in it a more modest working.

DUKE FREDERICK You shall try but one fall. 200

CHARLES No, I warrant your Grace you shall not entreat him to a second that have so mightily persuaded him from a first.

ORLANDO You mean to mock me after. You should not have mocked me before. But come your ways.

ROSALIND Now Hercules be thy speed, young man!

CELIA I would I were invisible, to catch the strong fellow by the leg.

45

[211] down *be thrown*

[214] breathed '*warmed up*'

[223] still *always*

[225] house *family*

[227] of another *that you had a different*

[230] calling *name and position in life*

[232] My father . . . as his soul *Note how our attitudes towards various characters are accurately influenced by their affection or dislike for the dead Sir Rowland.*
[233] was of . . . mind *agreed with him*
[235] unto *as well as*

ORLANDO and CHARLES *wrestle*

ROSALIND O excellent young man!

CELIA If I had a thunderbolt in mine eye, I can tell 210
who should down.

CHARLES *is thrown. Shout.*

DUKE FREDERICK No more, no more.

ORLANDO Yes, I beseech your Grace; I am not yet
well breathed.

DUKE FREDERICK How dost thou, Charles?

LE BEAU He cannot speak, my lord.

DUKE FREDERICK Bear him away. What is thy name,
young man?

ORLANDO Orlando, my liege, the youngest son of Sir
Rowland de Boys.   220

DUKE FREDERICK I would thou hadst been son to some
man else.
The world esteemed thy father honourable,
But I did find him still mine enemy.
Thou shouldst have better pleased me with this
deed
Hadst thou descended from another house.
But fare thee well; thou art a gallant youth;
I would thou hadst told me of another father.

[*Exit* DUKE, *with* LE BEAU, TOUCHSTONE *and* LORDS

CELIA Were I my father, coz, would I do this?

ORLANDO I am more proud to be Sir Rowland's son,
His youngest son, and would not change that
calling   230
To be adopted heir to Frederick.

ROSALIND My father loved Sir Rowland as his soul
And all the world was of my father's mind.
Had I before known this young man his son,
I should have given him tears unto entreaties
Ere he should thus have ventured.

[239] Sticks . . . heart *pains my heart*

[241] justly *exactly*

[243] out of suits *out of favour*
[244] could give *would like to give*

[246–7] parts . . . thrown down *qualities are all overcome*

[248] quintain *a post or figure used in tilting-practice*

[250] would *wishes*

[253] Have with you *I'm coming*

[255] urged conference *invited conversation*

[257] Or *Either*
something weaker *i.e. a woman*
[258] counsel *advise*

[261] condition *mood, disposition*
[262] misconsters *misinterprets*

CELIA   Gentle cousin,
    Let us go thank him and encourage him.
    My father's rough and envious disposition
    Sticks me at heart. Sir, you have well deserved;
    If you do keep your promises in love   240
    But justly as you have exceeded all promise,
    Your mistress shall be happy.
ROSALIND   Gentleman, [*gives him a chain*]
    Wear this for me, one out of suits with fortune,
    That could give more but that her hand lacks
        means.
    Shall we go, coz?
CELIA   Ay. Fare you well, fair gentleman.
ORLANDO   Can I not say 'I thank you'? My better
        parts
    Are all thrown down, and that which here stands
        up
    Is but a quintain, a mere lifeless block.
ROSALIND   He calls us back. My pride fell with my
        fortunes;
    I'll ask him what he would. Did you call, sir?   250
    Sir, you have wrestled well, and overthrown
    More than your enemies.
CELIA   Will you go, coz?
ROSALIND   Have with you. [*To* ORLANDO] Fare you
    well.   [*Exeunt* ROSALIND *and* CELIA
ORLANDO   What passion hangs these weights upon my
        tongue?
    I cannot speak to her, yet she urged conference.
                    Enter LE BEAU
    O poor Orlando, thou art overthrown!
    Or Charles or something weaker masters thee.
LE BEAU   Good sir, I do in friendship counsel you
    To leave this place. Albeit you have deserved
    High commendation, true applause, and love,   260
    Yet such is now the Duke's condition
    That he misconsters all that you have done.

49

[263] humorous *moody. Man's nature was held to be formed of four 'humours' which should be kept in balance in a normal person. Predominance of any one 'humour' led to various excesses of behaviour. The word retains some of its former meaning when we talk of a person as being in a 'good' or 'bad' humour.*

[264] More . . . conceive *it is better for you to understand by my implications*

[269] taller . . . daughter *Elsewhere Rosalind is said to be taller than Celia. This reference is probably either a printer's error or an uncorrected alteration made for a particular performance.*

[272] whose loves *their loves*

[276-7] Grounded . . . virtues *Compare this with Oliver's expressed reasons for disliking Orlando.*

[276] argument *reason*

[279] on my life *I'll stake my life on it*

[281] in a better . . . this *in better times than these*

[283] bounden *indebted*

[284] smother *thicker smoke: 'out of the frying pan into the fire'. The line emphasises the similarities between Duke Frederick and Oliver: both families in the court world are governed by envious and malicious tyrants; Orlando is himself concerned with both.*

[286] heavenly Rosalind! *an open acknowledgement of love, which outweighs Orlando's sense of danger*

ACT ONE, scene 3
The flight of Orlando is now followed by the banishment of Rosalind, and her flight with Celia. All three recover their good spirits rapidly after adverse treatment, and their disappearance from the court means that it is deprived of the only attractive persons we have seen in it, and is abandoned to tyranny and spite.

[1-25] Why cousin . . . despite of a fall *At first we see Rosalind dejected, contrasting with Orlando's romantic elation at the end of Scene 2. However, Rosalind quickly responds to Celia's banter, which opens with a reference to the love-god Cupid and so goes straight to the question of Rosalind's new-found affection. Celia's role in the play is often underrated – notice the effect she has on Rosalind here.*

[9] mad *melancholy*

The Duke is humorous. What he is, indeed,
More suits you to conceive than I to speak of.

ORLANDO I thank you, sir; and pray you, tell me this:
Which of the two was daughter of the Duke,
That here was at the wrestling?

LE BEAU Neither his daughter, if we judge by
  manners,
But yet indeed the taller is his daughter;
The other is daughter to the banished Duke, 270
And here detained by her usurping uncle
To keep his daughter company, whose loves
Are dearer than the natural bond of sisters.
But I can tell you that of late this Duke
Hath ta'en displeasure 'gainst his gentle niece,
Grounded upon no other argument
But that the people praise her for her virtues
And pity her for her good father's sake;
And, on my life, his malice 'gainst the lady
Will suddenly break forth. Sir, fare you well. 280
Hereafter, in a better world than this,
I shall desire more love and knowledge of you.

ORLANDO I rest much bounden to you. Fare you well.
              [Exit LE BEAU
Thus must I from the smoke into the smother,
From tyrant Duke unto a tyrant brother.
But heavenly Rosalind!   [Exit

Scene 3. *Enter* CELIA *and* ROSALIND

CELIA Why, cousin, why, Rosalind! Cupid have
  mercy, not a word?

ROSALIND Not one to throw at a dog.

CELIA No, thy words are too precious to be cast away
  upon curs; throw some of them at me. Come, lame
  me with reasons.

ROSALIND Then there were two cousins laid up, when
  the one should be lamed with reasons and the other
  mad without any.

[11] my child's father *i.e. Orlando (she hopes!) – a frank admission of her love*

[12] briars *sudden changes of circumstance (especially those brought about by falling in love). A further sudden change is to overtake Rosalind by the end of this scene.*

working-day world *everyday life; but also the world of the court, shortly to be contrasted with that of the forest*

[14–15] trodden paths *Celia is suggesting that Rosalind's feelings are just a momentary hurt, brought about by their indiscretion in leaving the 'trodden paths' of customary behaviour to talk with Orlando.*

[18] Hem *(i) Cough; (ii) Sew them up*

[19] cry 'hem' *clear my throat. Rosalind puns on 'hem' and 'him'.*

[21] wrestle . . . affections *Note how Celia provides a cue for Rosalind.*

[24] a good . . . upon you *good luck to you*

try *i.e. try a bout of wrestling with Orlando*

[25] in despite . . . fall *(i) notwithstanding your having fallen in love already; (ii) in defiance of the sexual consequences*

[25–6] turning . . . service *Having improved Rosalind's mood by jesting, Celia gets down to business.*

[29] The Duke . . . dearly *an evasive reply which Celia treats unmercifully*

[31] chase *(i) sequence of argument; (ii) pursuit*

[32] dearly *intensely*

[35] deserve well *deserve to be hated. This is the logical outcome of Rosalind's reasoning.*

[39] your . . . haste *as much speed as you safely can*

[40] cousin *kinswoman. The word is used here in its general sense.*

CELIA   But is all this for your father?   10

ROSALIND   No, some of it is for my child's father. O,   > Orlando
  how full of briars is this working-day world!

CELIA   They are but burrs, cousin, thrown upon thee
  in holiday foolery; if we walk not in the trodden
  paths, our very petticoats will catch them.

ROSALIND   I could shake them off my coat; these burrs
  are in my heart.

CELIA   Hem them away.

ROSALIND   I would try, if I could cry 'hem,' and have
  him.   20

CELIA   Come, come, wrestle with thy affections.

ROSALIND   O, they take the part of a better wrestler
  than myself!

CELIA   O, a good wish upon you! You will try in time,
  in despite of a fall. But turning these jests out of
  service, let us talk in good earnest. Is it possible on
  such a sudden you should fall into so strong a liking
  with old Sir Rowland's youngest son?

ROSALIND   The Duke my father loved his father dearly.

CELIA   Doth it therefore ensue that you should love   30
  his son dearly? By this kind of chase, I should hate
  him, for my father hated his father dearly; yet I hate
  not Orlando.

ROSALIND   No, faith, hate him not, for my sake.

CELIA   Why should I not? Doth he not deserve well?

Enter DUKE FREDERICK, *with* LORDS

ROSALIND   Let me love him for that, and do you love
  him because I do. Look, here comes the Duke.

CELIA   With his eyes full of anger.

DUKE FREDERICK   Mistress, dispatch you with your
    safest haste
And get you from our court.

ROSALIND   Me, uncle?

DUKE FREDERICK   You, cousin.   40
    Within these ten days if that thou beest found

[45] myself . . . intelligence *understand my own mind and thoughts*

[47] frantic *mad*

[51] purgation *proof of innocence (referring to the establishment of innocence in law, both by the declaration of an oath and by the undergoing of ordeal)*

[53] Let . . . trust thee not *In short, the Duke is acting on irrational impulse.*

[55] whereon *on what grounds*

[60] friends *relations (an obsolete use of the word)*

[61] What's that . . . me? *What has that to do with me?*

[63] To think . . . treacherous *To think I am a traitor just because I am poor*

[65] stayed *kept*

[66] ranged *wandered*

[68] remorse *compassion*

[71] still *always*

So near our public court as twenty miles,
Thou diest for it.

ROSALIND   I do beseech your Grace
  Let me the knowledge of my fault bear with
   me.
  If with myself I hold intelligence
  Or have acquaintance with mine own desires,
  If that I do not dream or be not frantic –
  As I do trust I am not – then, dear uncle,
  Never so much as in a thought unborn
  Did I offend your Highness.

DUKE FREDERICK   Thus do all traitors.   50
  If their purgation did consist in words,
  They are as innocent as grace itself.
  Let it suffice thee that I trust thee not.

ROSALIND   Yet your mistrust cannot make me a
  traitor.
  Tell me whereon the likelihoods depends.

DUKE FREDERICK   Thou art thy father's daughter,
  there's enough.

ROSALIND   So was I when your Highness took his
  dukedom;
  So was I when your Highness banished him.
  Treason is not inherited, my lord,
  Or, if we did derive it from our friends,   60
  What's that to me? My father was no traitor.
  Then, good my liege, mistake me not so much
  To think my poverty is treacherous.

CELIA   Dear sovereign, hear me speak.

DUKE FREDERICK   Ay, Celia. We stayed her for your
  sake,
  Else had she with her father ranged along.

CELIA   I did not then entreat to have her stay;
  It was your pleasure and your own remorse.
  I was too young that time to value her,
  But now I know her. If she be a traitor,   70
  Why, so am I. We still have slept together,

[73] Juno's swans *Traditionally swans were associated with Venus, and peacocks with Juno.*

[74] Still . . . inseparable *Celia's dignified insistence on her sisterly association and equality with Rosalind contrasts sharply with the jealous concern for differences and obsession with public opinion which Duke Frederick goes on to express, and which echoes Oliver's reasons for detesting Orlando.*

[75] subtle *crafty*

[75–7] her smoothness . . . pity her *These lines associate our impressions of Rosalind and Orlando. Both are envied and ill-treated; both are admired by the wider, unseen public, which is shown to be correct in its judgements. The people also loved Sir Rowland de Boys. The reported accuracy of their opinions has the effect of making the villains, Oliver and Duke Frederick, appear unbalanced and isolated.*

[78] name *proper reputation*

[81] doom *sentence*

[85] provide yourself *make ready to go*

[87] greatness *power*

[94–5] Rosalind lacks . . . am one *Celia now proves in adversity the truth of her earlier protestations.*

Rose at an instant, learned, played, eat
together;
And wheresoe'er we went, like Juno's swans,
Still we went coupled and inseparable.

DUKE FREDERICK   She is too subtle for thee; and her
smoothness,
Her very silence and her patience,
Speak to the people, and they pity her.
Thou art a fool. She robs thee of thy name,
And thou wilt show more bright and seem more
virtuous
When she is gone. Then open not thy lips.   80
Firm and irrevocable is my doom
Which I have passed upon her; she is banished.

CELIA   Pronounce that sentence then on me, my liege;
I cannot live out of her company.

DUKE FREDERICK   You are a fool. You, niece, provide
yourself;
If you outstay the time, upon mine honour
And in the greatness of my word, you die.

                                [*Exit* DUKE, *with* LORDS

CELIA   O my poor Rosalind, whither wilt thou go?
Wilt thou change fathers? I will give thee mine.
I charge thee, be not thou more grieved than I
am.   90

ROSALIND   I have more cause.

CELIA   Thou hast not, cousin.
Prithee be cheerful. Know'st thou not the
Duke
Hath banished me, his daughter?

ROSALIND   That he hath not.

CELIA   No? Hath not? Rosalind lacks then the love
Which teacheth thee that thou and I am one.
Shall we be sundered? Shall we part, sweet
girl?
No, let my father seek another heir.
Therefore devise with me how we may fly,

[100] take . . . upon you *shoulder the burden of your changed fortunes*

[102] now . . . pale *now pale in sympathy with our grief*

[110] umber *brown earth. Elizabethan ladies did not share the modern liking for a healthy tan, and the white, protected skins of Rosalind and Celia would be conspicuous in the countryside.*

[111] The like . . . you *You do the same*
pass along *go on our way*

[113] common *usually*

[114] suit . . . points *dress and equip myself in every way*

[115] curtle-axe *short sword*

[118] swashing . . . martial outside *swaggering and warlike appearance*

[119] mannish cowards *cowardly men*

[120] outface . . . semblances *rely on their (brave) appearance as a bluff*

[126] Aliena *the stranger*

[127] assayed *tried*

[131] woo *persuade*

Whither to go, and what to bear with us;
And do not seek to take your change upon you, 100
To bear your griefs yourself and leave me out;
For, by this heaven, now at our sorrows pale,
Say what thou canst, I'll go along with thee.

ROSALIND   Why, whither shall we go?

CELIA   To seek my uncle in the Forest of Arden.

ROSALIND   Alas, what danger will it be to us,
Maids as we are, to travel forth so far!
Beauty provoketh thieves sooner than gold.

CELIA   I'll put myself in poor and mean attire
And with a kind of umber smirch my face;   110
The like do you; so shall we pass along
And never stir assailants.

ROSALIND   Were it not better,
Because that I am more than common tall,
That I did suit me all points like a man?
A gallant curtle-axe upon my thigh,
A boar-spear in my hand; and, in my heart
Lie there what hidden woman's fear there
   will,
We'll have a swashing and a martial outside,
As many other mannish cowards have
That do outface it with their semblances.   120

CELIA   What shall I call thee when thou art a man?

ROSALIND   I'll have no worse a name than Jove's own
   page,
And therefore look you call me Ganymede.
But what will you be called?

CELIA   Something that hath a reference to my state:
No longer Celia, but Aliena.

ROSALIND   But, cousin, what if we assayed to steal
The clownish fool out of your father's court:
Would he not be a comfort to our travel?

CELIA   He'll go along o'er the wide world with me;   130
Leave me alone to woo him. Let's away
And get our jewels and our wealth together,

Devise the fittest time and safest way
To hide us from pursuit that will be made
After my flight. Now go in we content
To liberty, and not to banishment.

[*Exeunt*

ACT TWO, scene 1

The corruptions of court life are now contrasted with the Forest of Arden. Arden is not depicted as an idealised 'golden world', however. Duke Senior and his companions enact a courteous way of life which would typify an uncorrupted court, and does not depend on rustic simplicities. They endure the privations of a real forest in which summer is not perpetual. Nor does their carefree existence grant freedom from moral preoccupations, which are prominent in serious as well as comic forms.

[1] co-mates *companions*

[2] old custom *(i) our long familiarity with forest life; (ii) the civilised customs which forest life has regenerated*

[4] envious *Duke Senior singles out the chief characteristic of court life as we saw it in Act 1 – envy engenders direct hatred which imperils its victims.*

[5] Here feel . . . Adam *For a note on the text of this line, see Introduction, p. 22. The hardships of the forest are natural and seasonal, incurred by all men since the fall of Adam; they contrast favourably with the unnatural hardships of the court.*

[6] as *for example*

[7–10] chiding . . . flattery *The Duke contrasts the sincere rebuke to the body inflicted by cold winds, and the hypocritical flattery inflicted on the mind by fawning courtiers.*

[11] feelingly persuade me *instruct me through my senses*

[12] uses *benefits*

[13–14] toad . . . head *Toads were superstitiously believed (i) to be poisonous, and (ii) to contain in their heads a magical stone which counteracted poison.*

[15] exempt . . . haunt *free from intrusion*

[19] stubbornness *sustained hostility*

[20] style *a style both of living and of moral contemplation*

[22] irks me *troubles me that*
fools *simple creatures.* Not *the modern meaning.*

[23] burghers *townsfolk, citizens*
desert city *i.e. the forest*

[24] confines *territories*
forkèd heads *arrows*

ACT TWO

Scene 1. *Enter* DUKE SENIOR, AMIENS *and two or three*
LORDS, *dressed like foresters*

DUKE SENIOR   Now, my co-mates and brothers in exile,
Hath not old custom made this life more sweet
Than that of painted pomp? Are not these woods
More free from peril than the envious court?
Here feel we but the penalty of Adam,
The seasons' difference, as the icy fang
And churlish chiding of the winter's wind,
Which, when it bites and blows upon my body
Even till I shrink with cold, I smile and say
'This is no flattery; these are counsellors   10
That feelingly persuade me what I am.'
Sweet are the uses of adversity
Which, like the toad, ugly and venomous,
Wears yet a precious jewel in his head;
And this our life, exempt from public haunt,
Finds tongues in trees, books in the running
   brooks,
Sermons in stones, and good in everything.

AMIENS   I would not change it; happy is your Grace
That can translate the stubbornness of fortune
Into so quiet and so sweet a style.   20

DUKE SENIOR   Come, shall we go and kill us venison?
And yet it irks me the poor dappled fools,
Being native burghers of this desert city,
Should, in their own confines, with forkèd
   heads
Have their round haunches gored.

FIRST LORD   Indeed, my lord,
The melancholy Jaques grieves at that,
And in that kind swears you do more usurp
Than doth your brother that hath banished you.

[27] in that kind   *in that respect*

[27-8] more usurp . . . banished you   *The Duke has shown a sober and intelligent style of moral contemplation; this report on Jaques describes a man who carries the same processes of thought to ridiculous excess.*

[33] the which   *this*
     sequestered   *separated from the herd*

[40] piteous   *pitiful*
     fool   *simple creature*

[41] Much . . . of   *Closely observed by*

[43] Augmenting   *Adding to*

[44] moralize   *extract moral lessons from*

[46] needless   *i.e. not in need of additional water*

[47-9] thou mak'st . . . too much   *you are making a will in which, like worldly people, you bequeath more to those who are already too rich*

[50] of   *by*
     velvet   *soft-coated. The deer is abandoned by the herd, not Jaques by the deer.*

[51-2] part . . . company   *separate the miserable one from the throng*

[52] Anon   *Presently*
     careless   *carefree*

[53] Full of the pasture   *Well-fed*
     him   *i.e. the injured deer*

[58-9] Thus . . . court   *Thus he vehemently attacks the state of the country, the city and the court. Although Jaques' moralising is exaggerated and marked by a somewhat theatrical bitterness, it does deter us from making absolute contrasts between court and country. Comparisons can be made, even if they risk absurdity.*

[61] mere   *nothing but*
     and what's worse   *and worse things still*

Today my Lord of Amiens and myself
Did steal behind him as he lay along   30
Under an oak, whose antique root peeps out
Upon the brook that brawls along this wood,
To the which place a poor sequestered stag
That from the hunter's aim had ta'en a hurt
Did come to languish; and indeed, my lord,
The wretched animal heaved forth such groans
That their discharge did stretch his leathern
     coat
Almost to bursting, and the big round tears
Coursed one another down his innocent nose
In piteous chase; and thus the hairy fool,   40
Much markèd of the melancholy Jaques,
Stood on th' extremest verge of the swift brook,
Augmenting it with tears.

DUKE SENIOR   But what said Jaques?
Did he not moralize this spectacle?

FIRST LORD   O, yes, into a thousand similes.
First, for his weeping into the needless stream:
'Poor deer,' quoth he, 'thou mak'st a testament
As worldlings do, giving thy sum of more
To that which had too much.' Then, being
     there alone,
Left and abandoned of his velvet friend: 50
''Tis right,', quoth he, 'thus misery doth part
The flux of company.' Anon a careless herd,
Full of the pasture, jumps along by him
And never stays to greet him: 'Ay,' quoth
     Jaques,
'Sweep on, you fat and greasy citizens,
'Tis just the fashion; wherefore do you look
Upon that poor and broken bankrupt there?'
Thus most invectively he pierceth through
The body of the country, city, court,
Yea, and of this our life, swearing that we   60
Are mere usurpers, tyrants, and what's worse,

[67] cope   *meet and tackle*
[68] matter   *things worth listening to*
[69] straight   *immediately*

ACT TWO, scene 2
A brief return to the court. This scene would be played on the recessed inner stage of the Elizabethan playhouse.

[3] Are of consent and sufferance in   *Have connived at*

[7] untreasured   *robbed of its treasure (i.e. Celia)*

[8] roynish   *scurvy, low, mean*

[9] wont   *accustomed*

[13] parts *qualities*
[14] foil   *defeat*

[17] that gallant   *i.e. Orlando*

[19] suddenly   *at once*

66

To fright the animals and to kill them up
In their assigned and native dwelling place.

DUKE SENIOR   And did you leave him in this
    contemplation?

SECOND LORD   We did, my lord, weeping and
    commenting
Upon the sobbing deer.

DUKE SENIOR   Show me the place.
I love to cope him in these sullen fits,
For then he's full of matter.

FIRST LORD   I'll bring you to him straight.

                                  [*Exeunt*

Scene 2. *Enter* DUKE FREDERICK, *with* LORDS

DUKE FREDERICK   Can it be possible that no man saw
    them?
It cannot be; some villains of my court
Are of consent and sufferance in this.

FIRST LORD   I cannot hear of any that did see her.
The ladies, her attendants of her chamber,
Saw her abed, and in the morning early
They found the bed untreasured of their
    mistress.

SECOND LORD   My lord, the roynish clown at whom so
    oft
Your Grace was wont to laugh is also missing.
Hisperia, the princess' gentlewoman,   10
Confesses that she secretly o'erheard
Your daughter and her cousin much commend
The parts and graces of the wrestler
That did but lately foil the sinewy Charles,
And she believes, wherever they are gone,
That youth is surely in their company.

DUKE FREDERICK   Send to his brother, fetch that
    gallant hither;
If he be absent, bring his brother to me;
I'll make him find him. Do this suddenly,

[20] let not . . . inquisition quail   *do not let search and enquiry slacken*

[21] bring again.   *bring back*

ACT TWO, scene 3

This scene advances the plot by depriving Orlando of sanctuary and finally exiling all virtue from the 'urban' world of the play. For the rest, its sheer concentration of human virtuousness perhaps supplies an over-sententious counterblast to the wickedness we see elsewhere. The scene reiterates the play's concern with abnormally violent envy.

[3–4] you memory . . . Rowland   *Once again the audience is reminded of Orlando's resemblance to his dead father, who is betrayed by Oliver, detested by Duke Frederick and liked and admired by everyone else.*

[3] memory   *memorial*

[4] what make you . . .?   *what are you doing . . .?*

[5–6] Why are you virtuous . . . valiant?   *Another reminder of the dangers inherent in personal qualities and public popularity.*

[7] so fond to   *so foolish as to*

[8] bonny prizer   *strong prize-fighter*

[12] No more do yours   *Your virtues serve you no better than theirs do*

[13] sanctified . . . traitors   *This paradox underlines the inverted morals of the court world, which are the opposite of a sane and normal moral order.*

[15] Envenoms   *'Poisons', or 'is regarded as poisonous'. The rest of the speech makes the second explanation more probable.*

[17] roof   *house*

[19–21] Your brother . . . his father   *Adam stresses Oliver's repudiation of the sacred ties and obligations of blood relationship.*

[23] use to lie   *are accustomed to sleep*

[25] cut you off   *kill you*

[26] practices   *plots*

[27] place   *home*

And let not search and inquisition quail 20
To bring again these foolish runaways.

         [*Exeunt*

Scene 3. *Enter* ORLANDO *and* ADAM

ORLANDO Who's there?
ADAM What, my young master, O my gentle master,
O my sweet master, O you memory
Of old Sir Rowland, why, what make you here?
Why are you virtuous? Why do people love you?
And wherefore are you gentle, strong, and
  valiant?
Why would you be so fond to overcome
The bonny prizer of the humorous Duke?
Your praise is come too swiftly home before you.
Know you not, master, to some kind of men 10
Their graces serve them but as enemies?
No more do yours. Your virtues, gentle master,
Are sanctified and holy traitors to you.
O, what a world is this, when what is comely
Envenoms him that bears it!
ORLANDO Why, what's the matter?
ADAM   O unhappy youth,
Come not within these doors; within this roof
The enemy of all your graces lives.
Your brother – no, no brother, yet the son –
Yet not the son, I will not call him son, 20
Of him I was about to call his father –
Hath heard your praises, and this night he
  means
To burn the lodging where you use to lie,
And you within it. If he fail of that,
He will have other means to cut you off.
I overheard him, and his practices.
This is no place, this house is but a butchery;
Abhor it, fear it, do not enter it!

[30] so   *provided that*

[32] boisterous   *violent*
[32–3] enforce . . . living   *get my living by force*

[37] diverted blood   *blood-relationship turned out of its natural course (involving loyalty and protection, qualities which Oliver denies and which Orlando will later show towards Oliver)*
[39] thrifty hire   *careful savings out of my wages*
[40] to . . . foster-nurse   *to support, and care for me*
[41] lie lame   *be crippled and unable to continue*
[42] thrown   *be thrown*
[43–4] he that doth . . . sparrow   *Various biblical sources have been suggested for these lines. Note particularly Psalm 147.9 and Matthew 10.29.*

[47] lusty   *vigorous*

[49] rebellious   *'causing rebellion within the body' or, less probably, 'causing me to behave rebelliously'*

[50–1] Nor did not . . . debility   *Nor did I ask for later weakness and ill-health by indulging in reckless pleasures*
[52] lusty   *hard*

[57] constant   *loyal*
    antique   *ancient. Another reference to the merit of ancient custom.*
[58] sweat   *sweated*
    meed   *reward*
[61] choke . . . up   *withdraw the services which caused them to be promoted*
[63] a rotten tree   *i.e. Orlando himself*

ORLANDO   Why, whither, Adam, wouldst thou have
   me go?

ADAM No matter whither, so you come not here.   30

ORLANDO What, wouldst thou have me go and beg
   my food,
   Or with a base and boisterous sword enforce
   A thievish living on the common road?
   This I must do, or know not what to do;
   Yet this I will not do, do how I can.
   I rather will subject me to the malice
   Of a diverted blood and bloody brother.

ADAM But do not so. I have five hundred crowns,
   The thrifty hire I saved under your father,
   Which I did store to be my foster nurse   40
   When service should in my old limbs lie lame
   And unregarded age in corners thrown.
   Take that, and he that doth the ravens feed,
   Yea, providently caters for the sparrow,
   Be comfort to my age. Here is the gold;
   All this I give you. Let me be your servant;
   Though I look old, yet I am strong and lusty,
   For in my youth I never did apply
   Hot and rebellious liquors in my blood,
   Nor did not with unbashful forehead woo   50
   The means of weakness and debility;
   Therefore my age is as a lusty winter,
   Frosty, but kindly. Let me go with you;
   I'll do the service of a younger man
   In all your business and necessities.

ORLANDO O good old man, how well in thee appears
   The constant service of the antique world,
   When service sweat for duty, not for meed!
   Thou art not for the fashion of these times,
   Where none will sweat but for promotion,   60
   And having that, do choke their service up
   Even with the having; it is not so with thee.
   But, poor old man, thou prun'st a rotten tree

[65] In lieu of *In return for*
    husbandry *careful tending*

[68] settled low content *settled, if humble, way of life which
will content us*
[70] truth *fidelity*

[74] too late a week '*too late in the day*'

ACT TWO, scene 4

*With this scene we begin in earnest the masquerade which
forms the centrepiece of the comedy, exerting an ever-widening
influence on events – Rosalind's disguise as the boy Ganymede.
We also see once again the dual nature of the Forest of Arden:
it is both an ideal pastoral world, containing such an absurdly
stricken lover as Silvius, and an actual forest, in which people
are afflicted with real fatigue and hunger.*

[4–5] I could find . . . woman *Confronted with comfortless
forest at the end of their tiring journey, the girls display a dejection
which is in comic contrast to their untutored exuberance before they
set out. Rosalind, for the first of many times, finds her masculine role
hard to keep up.*

[6] weaker vessel *i.e. the woman. Rosalind comments wryly
on the responsibilities her disguise confers on her.*
    doublet and hose *jacket and breeches*

[10–11] I had rather . . . bear you *I would rather be patient
with you than carry you*

[11] no cross *(i) no trouble; (ii) no money. An allusion to coins
which were stamped with a cross. The pun was commonplace.*

[15–17] Ay, now am I . . . content *The dry realism and dis-
illusionment of Touchstone contrasts with Duke Senior's idealisation
of the forest in Act 2, Scene 1.*

That cannot so much as a blossom yield
In lieu of all thy pains and husbandry.
But come thy ways, we'll go along together,
And ere we have thy youthful wages spent,
We'll light upon some settled low content.

ADAM   Master, go on, and I will follow thee
To the last gasp with truth and loyalty.   70
From seventeen years till now almost fourscore
Here livèd I, but now live here no more:
At seventeen years many their fortunes seek,
But at fourscore it is too late a week;
Yet fortune cannot recompense me better
Than to die well, and not my master's debtor.
                                                    [Exeunt

Scene 4. *Enter* ROSALIND *as Ganymede,* CELIA *as Aliena
and* TOUCHSTONE

ROSALIND   O Jupiter, how weary are my spirits!

TOUCHSTONE   I care not for my spirits if my legs were
    not weary.

ROSALIND   I could find in my heart to disgrace my
    man's apparel and to cry like a woman; but I must
    comfort the weaker vessel, as doublet and hose
    ought to show itself courageous to petticoat. There-
    fore, courage, good Aliena!

CELIA   I pray you bear with me; I cannot go no further.

TOUCHSTONE   For my part, I had rather bear with you   10
    than bear you: yet I should bear no cross if I did
    bear you, for I think you have no money in your
    purse.

ROSALIND   Well, this is the Forest of Arden.

TOUCHSTONE   Ay, now am I in Arden, the more fool I.
    When I was at home I was in a better place, but
    travellers must be content.

Enter CORIN *and* SILVIUS

ROSALIND   Ay, be so, good Touchstone. Look you,

[23] partly   *to some extent*

[25] Though   *Even though*
[26] As ever . . . pillow   *As ever lay sleepless with frustrated love*

[29] How many . . . ridiculous   *The comic absurdity of lovers'
behaviour is one of the play's chief preoccupations. Rosalind has
already touched on it, with characteristic self-knowledge, and Sylvius
now restates the idea.*
  [30] drawn to   *drawn into*
      fantasy   *affection*

[37] Wearing   *Tiring*
      in thy mistress' praise   *by praising your loved one*

[43] Searching of   *Probing*

[44] hard adventure   *ill-luck*

[45–55] And I mine . . . mortal in folly   *The spectacle of two
distressed lovers is too much for Touchstone, who joins in the act with
a mocking account of his own ridiculous affair.*

  [48] batler   *wooden beater used in washing clothes*
  [49] chopt   *chapped*
  [50] peascod   *pea-pod (connected with courtship in rural
superstitions)*

who comes here: a young man and an old in solemn
talk. 20

CORIN That is the way to make her scorn you still.

SILVIUS O Corin, that thou knew'st how I do love
her!

CORIN I partly guess, for I have loved ere now.

SILVIUS No, Corin, being old, thou canst not guess,
Though in thy youth thou wast as true a lover
As ever sighed upon a midnight pillow.
But if thy love were ever like to mine –
As sure I think did never man love so –
How many actions most ridiculous
Hast thou been drawn to by thy fantasy? 30

CORIN Into a thousand that I have forgotten.

SILVIUS O, thou didst then never love so heartily!
If thou rememb'rest not the slightest folly
That ever love did make thee run into,
Thou hast not loved.
Or if thou hast not sat as I do now,
Wearing thy hearer in thy mistress' praise,
Thou hast not loved.
Or if thou hast not broke from company
Abruptly, as my passion now makes me, 40
Thou hast not loved.
O Phebe, Phebe, Phebe!   [*Exit*

ROSALIND Alas, poor shepherd! Searching of thy
wound,
I have by hard adventure found mine own.

TOUCHSTONE And I mine. I remember, when I was
in love I broke my sword upon a stone and bid him
take that for coming a-night to Jane Smile; and I
remember the kissing of her batler, and the cow's
dugs that her pretty chopt hands had milked; and I
remember the wooing of a peascod instead of her, 50
from whom I took two cods and, giving her them
again, said with weeping tears, 'Wear these for my
sake.' We that are true lovers run into strange

75

[54–5] as all is mortal . . . folly *as everything that lives must die, so every living thing that loves is bound to behave foolishly*

[56] ware *aware*

[57] ware *Touchstone plays on the word, taking it to mean 'cautious'.*

[59–60] Jove . . . fashion *In these trite lines of verse Rosalind may be poking fun at Silvius' style of lamentation.*

[61] something *somewhat*

[67] Peace, fool *Rosalind sets out to control Touchstone as soon as his wit involves discourtesy to a stranger. But she does so by playing on words in Touchstone's own manner. He used 'clown' to mean 'rustic'. She takes it to mean 'fool', and hence a relative of the fool Touchstone.*

[69] even *evening*

[72] entertainment *food and shelter*

[73] Bring us *Take us*

[74] travail *wearying effort*

[75] for succour *for lack of help*

[79] do not shear . . . graze *do not collect the profits of my work*

[81] recks to find *cares about finding*

[83] cote *cottage*
bounds of feed *entire pastures*

[84] on sale *being sold*

[86] what is *what there is*

capers; but as all is mortal in nature, so is all nature
in love mortal in folly.

ROSALIND   Thou speakest wiser than thou art ware of.

TOUCHSTONE   Nay, I shall ne'er be ware of mine own
wit till I break my shins against it.

ROSALIND   Jove, Jove! This shepherd's passion
     Is much upon my fashion.   *makes her become emotional*   60

TOUCHSTONE   And mine, but it grows something stale
with me.

CELIA   I pray you, one of you question yond man
     If he for gold will give us any food.
     I faint almost to death.

TOUCHSTONE   Holla, you clown!   *sneering*

ROSALIND   Peace, fool! He's not thy kinsman.

CORIN   Who calls?

TOUCHSTONE   Your betters, sir.

CORIN   Else are they very wretched.

ROSALIND   Peace, I say! Good even to you, friend.

CORIN   And to you, gentle sir, and to you all.   70

ROSALIND   I prithee, shepherd, if that love or gold
     Can in this desert place buy entertainment,
     Bring us where we may rest ourselves and feed.
     Here's a young maid with travail much
          oppressed,
     And faints for succour.

CORIN   Fair sir, I pity her,
     And wish, for her sake more than for mine own,
     My fortunes were more able to relieve her;
     But I am shepherd to another man
     And do not shear the fleeces that I graze.
     My master is of churlish disposition   80
     And little recks to find the way to heaven
     By doing deeds of hospitality.
     Besides, his cote, his flocks, and bounds of feed
     Are now on sale, and at our sheepcote now,
     By reason of his absence, there is nothing
     That you will feed on. But what is, come see,

[87] in my voice   *so far as I have any say in things*
[88] What   *Who*

[89] but erewhile   *just a short time ago*

[91] stand with honesty   *is compatible with honest dealing*

[93] have to pay ... us   *have the cost of it from us*
[94] mend   *increase*
[95] waste   *spend*

[97] upon report   *on discovering more details*

[99] feeder   *servant*
[100] suddenly   *immediately*

ACT TWO, scene 5
Amiens' song recalls the greenwood life which Duke Senior praised at the beginning of Act 2 – a life of ease and fellowship, its rigours confined to wintry weather. We now meet the extensively reported Jaques, and experience his well-cultivated misanthropy, bluntness and mockery at first hand.

[3] turn   *adapt*

[15] ragged   *hoarse*

And in my voice most welcome shall you be.

ROSALIND What is he that shall buy his flock and
pasture?

CORIN That young swain that you saw here but
erewhile,
That little cares for buying anything. 90

ROSALIND I pray thee, if it stand with honesty,
Buy thou the cottage, pasture, and the flock,
And thou shalt have to pay for it of us.

CELIA And we will mend thy wages. I like this place,
And willingly could waste my time in it.

CORIN Assuredly the thing is to be sold.
Go with me; if you like upon report
The soil, the profit, and this kind of life,
I will your very faithful feeder be
And buy it with your gold right suddenly. 100

[*Exeunt*

Scene 5. *Enter* AMIENS, JAQUES *and others*

AMIENS [*Sings*]
          Under the greenwood tree
            Who loves to lie with me,
          And turn his merry note
            Unto the sweet bird's throat,
        Come hither, come hither, come hither.
            Here shall he see
            No enemy
          But winter and rough weather.

JAQUES More, more, I prithee more!

AMIENS It will make you melancholy, Monsieur 10
Jaques.

JAQUES I thank it. More, I prithee, more! I can suck
melancholy out of a song as a weasel sucks eggs.
More, I prithee, more!

AMIENS My voice is ragged. I know I cannot please
you.

JAQUES I do not desire you to please me; I do desire

[18] stanzo *stanza. The word was a recent acquisition in English, and Jaques mocks it as an affectation.*

[20] What you will *Whatever you like*

[21–2] Nay, I care not . . . nothing *Jaques quibbles on 'names', taking the word to mean the signature on a legal document admitting a debt.*

[25] that *that which*
      compliment *politeness*
[26] dog-apes *baboons*

[28] beggarly thanks *profuse thanks, like a beggar's*

[30] cover the while *in the meantime lay the table*

[32] look *look for*

[34] disputable *argumentative*

[45] note *tune*
[46] in despite . . . invention *without needing to use my imagination (which, by implication, is not needed to compose such nonsense)*

[53] Ducdame *Possible explanations of this word have been derived from various languages, including Romany and Latin. Most probably the word is deliberate nonsense. Jaques uses it as a deliberately mystifying word while he simultaneously beckons the company into a circle, so that when he is called upon to explain it he can characterise them as 'fools'. The nonsense is a trap, and they fall for it.*

you to sing. Come, more, another stanzo! Call you
'em 'stanzos'?

AMIENS   What you will, Monsieur Jaques.   20

JAQUES   Nay, I care not for their names; they owe me
nothing. Will you sing?

AMIENS   More at your request than to please myself.

JAQUES   Well then, if ever I thank any man, I'll thank
you. But that they call compliment is like th' encounter of two dog-apes, and when a man thanks me
heartily, methinks I have given him a penny and he
renders me the beggarly thanks. Come, sing; and
you that will not, hold your tongues.

AMIENS   Well, I'll end the song. Sirs, cover the while;   30
the Duke will drink under this tree. He hath been all
this day to look you.

JAQUES   And I have been all this day to avoid him. He
is too disputable for my company. I think of as many
matters as he, but I give heaven thanks and make no
boast of them. Come, warble, come.

ALL TOGETHER [*Sing*]

   Who doth ambition shun
    And loves to live i' th' sun,
   Seeking the food he eats,
    And pleased with what he gets,   40
  Come hither, come hither, come hither.
    Here shall he see
    No enemy
    But winter and rough weather.

JAQUES   I'll give you a verse to this note that I made
yesterday in despite of my invention.

AMIENS   And I'll sing it.

JAQUES   Thus it goes.

   If it do come to pass
   That any man turn ass,   50
   Leaving his wealth and ease
   A stubborn will to please,
   Ducdame, ducdame, ducdame.

[56] An if *If*

[58] Greek *meaningless*

[60] first-born of Egypt *See Exodus 11.5 and 12.12 and 29. Jaques appears to be making an obscure comparison between the Duke's banishment into the hardships of Arden, and the Israelites' journey into the wilderness after the first-born of Egypt had been destroyed by the Lord.*

[61] banquet *light meal, especially of fruit*

ACT TWO, scene 6

A brief connecting scene, bringing Orlando into the Forest of Arden. This scene would be played at the front of the Elizabethan stage, the Duke's 'banquet' remaining visible at the rear.

[1–2] for food *for lack of food*

[5] comfort *comfort yourself*

[6] uncouth *wild*

[8] Thy conceit . . . powers *You imagine yourself closer to death than you really are*

[9] comfortable *comforted, cheered*

[9–10] at the arm's end *at arm's length*

[10] presently *immediately*

[12–13] if thou diest . . . labour *Orlando has to accept his fair share of romantic absurdity, but in this brief scene his encouraging humour and spirited unselfishness show his personality akin to Rosalind's.*

[13] Well said *Well done!*

[17] desert *desolate place*
      Cheerly *Cheerfully*

ACT TWO, scene 7

This scene is characteristic of Shakespearean comedy at its most complex. It is dominated by Jaques, who is sceptical about mankind, and envies the fool his licence to attack human failings, and it ends with the sadness of Amiens' music. Yet the drift of its events is benign and optimistic, reaffirming the major courtly virtues and practices in spite of hardship and exile. The simple dignity of the Duke's feast, and his ready hospitality, are central to the effect.

   Here shall he see
   Gross fools as he
   An if he will come to me.

AMIENS What's that 'ducdame'?

JAQUES 'Tis a Greek invocation to call fools into a circle. I'll go sleep, if I can; if I cannot, I'll rail against all the first-born of Egypt.   60

AMIENS And I'll go seek the Duke. His banquet is prepared.   [*Exeunt*

Scene 6. *Enter* ORLANDO *and* ADAM

ADAM Dear master, I can go no further. O, I die for food. Here lie I down and measure out my grave. Farewell, kind master.

ORLANDO Why, how now, Adam? No greater heart in thee? Live a little, comfort a little, cheer thyself a little. If this uncouth forest yield anything savage, I will either be food for it or bring it for food to thee. Thy conceit is nearer death than thy powers. For my sake be comfortable; hold death awhile at the arm's end. I will here be with thee presently, and if 10 I bring thee not something to eat, I will give thee leave to die; but if thou diest before I come, thou art a mocker of my labour. Well said; thou lookest cheerly, and I'll be with thee quickly. Yet thou liest in the bleak air. Come, I will bear thee to some shelter, and thou shalt not die for lack of a dinner if there live anything in this desert. Cheerly, good Adam!   [*Exeunt*

Scene 7. *Enter* DUKE SENIOR *and* LORDS *dressed as foresters, or outlaws*

DUKE SENIOR I think he be transformed into a beast,
   For I can nowhere find him like a man.

FIRST LORD My lord, he is but even now gone hence;
   Here was he merry, hearing of a song.

[2] like   *in the appearance of*

[3] but even now   *only a moment ago*

[5] compact of jars   *made up of discords*

[6] discord in the spheres   *universal disorder. According to ancient astronomy, the planets produced harmonious music as they revolved, and this melody would need to become discordant before such as Jaques could become musical.*

[11] you look merrily?   *This is just as surprising as Jaques' reported delight in music!*

[13] A motley fool!   *A fool (i.e. Touchstone) in his multicoloured professional costume*

[16] railed on   *criticised*

[17] good set terms   *eloquent and precise language*

[19] Call me . . . fortune   *Fortune was supposed to favour fools, but Touchstone is still awaiting his.*

[20] dial   *(i) watch; (ii) pocket sun-dial*
     poke   *pocket*

[23] wags   *goes*

[27] hour to hour   *Touchstone is probably punning on 'hour' and 'whore', in which case 'tale' is also an indecent pun.*

[29] moral on   *philosophical about*

[30] crow . . . Chanticleer   *laugh like a crowing cock*

[32] sans intermission   *without pause*

[34] Motley's . . . wear   *A fool's outfit is the only garb worth wearing*

DUKE SENIOR   If he, compact of jars, grow musical,
        We shall have shortly discord in the spheres.
        Go seek him; tell him I would speak with him.

Enter JAQUES

FIRST LORD   He saves my labour by his own approach.

DUKE SENIOR   Why, how now, monsieur, what a life is
        this,
        That your poor friends must woo your
        company?   10
        What, you look merrily?

JAQUES   A fool! a fool! I met a fool i' th' forest,
        A motley fool! A miserable world!
        As I do live by food, I met a fool,
        Who laid him down and basked him in the sun,
        And railed on Lady Fortune in good terms,
        In good set terms, and yet a motley fool.
        'Good morrow, fool,' quoth I. 'No, sir,' quoth
        he,
        'Call me not fool till heaven hath sent me
        fortune.'
        And then he drew a dial from his poke,   20
        And looking on it with lack-lustre eye,
        Says very wisely, 'It is ten o'clock.
        Thus we may see,' quoth he, 'how the world
        wags.
        'Tis but an hour ago since it was nine,
        And after one hour more 'twill be eleven;
        And so, from hour to hour, we ripe and ripe,
        And then, from hour to hour, we rot and rot;
        And thereby hangs a tale.' When I did hear
        The motley fool thus moral on the time,
        My lungs began to crow like Chanticleer   30
        That fools should be so deep contemplative;
        And I did laugh, sans intermission,
        An hour by his dial. O noble fool,
        A worthy fool! Motley's the only wear.

[39] remainder biscuit   *dry biscuit left over at the end of a voyage. Nothing could be much drier or harder than that. A 'dry' brain was associated for the Elizabethans with a retentive memory.*

[40] places   *both 'places in his brain' and 'quotations learned by heart'*

[41] vents   *delivers*

[44] suit   *a pun: (i) dress; (ii) petition*

[45] weed   *a pun on weed: (i) clear (verb); (ii) clothing (noun)*

[46] rank   *overgrown (in turn suggested by 'weed')*

[48] Withal   *With it*
   large a charter   *generous licence*

[50] gallèd   *chafed, 'rubbed up the wrong way'*

[53] He that . . . hit   *The man who is criticised in the comments of a shrewd fool*

[55] senseless . . . bob   *unaware of the taunt*

[56] anatomized   *exposed and dissected*

[57] squandering glances   *random hits*

[58–61] Invest . . . medicine   *The satirist, whose role Jaques is adopting, habitually defended his work on the grounds that it was a distasteful but curative medicine.*
   - Invest   *Clothe*

[63] for a counter   *in exchange for a worthless coin (in payment for the information)*

[66] brutish sting   *animal lust*

DUKE SENIOR   What fool is this?

JAQUES   O worthy fool! One that hath been a courtier,
And says, if ladies be but young and fair,
They have the gift to know it. And in his brain,
Which is as dry as the remainder biscuit
After a voyage, he hath strange places crammed   40
With observation, the which he vents
In mangled forms. O that I were a fool!
I am ambitious for a motley coat.

DUKE SENIOR   Thou shalt have one.

JAQUES   It is my only suit,
Provided that you weed your better judgements
Of all opinion that grows rank in them
That I am wise. I must have liberty
Withal, as large a charter as the wind,
To blow on whom I please, for so fools have.
And they that are most gallèd with my folly,   50
They most must laugh. And why, sir, must they
   so?
The why is plain as way to parish church:
He that a fool doth very wisely hit
Doth very foolishly, although he smart,
Not to seem senseless of the bob. If not,
The wise man's folly is anatomized
Even by the squandering glances of the fool.
Invest me in my motley; give me leave
To speak my mind, and I will through and
   through
Cleanse the foul body of th' infected world,   60
If they will patiently receive my medicine.

DUKE SENIOR   Fie on thee! I can tell what thou wouldst
   do.

JAQUES   What, for a counter, would I do but good?

DUKE SENIOR   Most mischievous foul sin, in chiding
   sin:
For thou thyself hast been a libertine,
As sensual as the brutish sting itself;

[67] embossed . . . evils *swollen and protruding s ores and boils*

[68] licence . . . foot *free living. The power of the imagery cons ti-tutes a major attack by the Duke on Jaques' hypocrisy. He has enjoyed already the freedom he requests, and has used it to indulge the sins he now wishes to condemn. The would-be 'healer' is disgustingly sick.*

[70] Why, who cries out . . . *Jaques' reply is basically that satirical abuse is generally aimed, and only applies to individuals 'if the cap fits'.*

[71] tax . . . party *be held to criticise anyone in particular*

[73] Till that . . . ebb *A difficult line. Probably: 'Till the wealth on which pride depends is exhausted, and ebbs like the tide'.*

[76] cost of *wealth required to support*

[78] such a one . . . neighbour *her neighbour is just like her*

[79–80] what is he . . . cost *what meanly-employed person is there who replies that his fine clothes are not paid for by me (and there-fore are none of my business)*

[81–2] suits . . . speech *reveals himself as the kind of fool I have described*

[82] mettle *substance*

[84] do him right *describes him correctly*

[85] free *innocent*

[86] taxing *criticism*

[89] necessity *the person in extreme need*

[93] civility *courtesy*

[94] You touched . . . first *Your first description of my state of mind was right*

[96] inland bred *brought up near centres of civilisation*

  And all th' embossed sores and headed evils
  That thou with licence of free foot hast caught,
  Wouldst thou disgorge into the general world.
JAQUES Why, who cries out on pride   70
  That can therein tax any private party?
  Doth it not flow as hugely as the sea
  Till that the weary very means do ebb?
  What woman in the city do I name
  When that I say the city woman bears
  The cost of princes on unworthy shoulders?
  Who can come in and say that I mean her,
  When such a one as she, such is her neighbour?
  Or what is he of basest function
  That says his bravery is not on my cost, 80
  Thinking that I mean him, but therein suits
  His folly to the mettle of my speech?
  There then, how then, what then? Let me see
   wherein
  My tongue hath wronged him. If it do him right,
  Then he hath wronged himself. If he be free,
  Why, then my taxing like a wild goose flies,
  Unclaimed of any man. But who comes here?

   Enter ORLANDO *with drawn sword*

ORLANDO Forbear, and eat no more!
JAQUES   Why, I have eat none yet.
ORLANDO Nor shalt not, till necessity be served.
JAQUES Of what kind should this cock come of? 90
DUKE SENIOR Art thou thus boldened, man, by thy
  distress,
  Or else a rude despiser of good manners,
  That in civility thou seem'st so empty?
ORLANDO You touched my vein at first. The thorny
  point
  Of bare distress hath ta'en from me the show
  Of smooth civility; yet am I inland bred

[97] nurture *culture, good breeding*

[99] answerèd *satisfied*

[100–1] An you . . . die *On stage it is usual for Jaques to take a bite at something as he says this.*

[100] An *If*

[102–3] Your gentleness . . . gentleness *Civilised behaviour will prompt a kind response in us more readily than will force*

[106] gently *like a gentleman*

[107] had been *would have been*

[108] countenance *appearance*

[110] desert *desolate place*

[112] Lose and neglect *Pass without concern*

[114] knolled *rung*

[118] Let gentleness . . . be *Let your gentle breeding support my request. In this speech Orlando bases his appeal on the customs and courtesies of civilised society, a reminder that these have been brought into the forest by the exiles and belong naturally in the world they have come from.*

[120–126] True is it . . . ministered *The Duke's formal repetition of the symbolic customs mentioned by Orlando has the effect of investing them with ceremonial importance.*

[125] upon command *at your will*

[126] wanting *necessity*

[128–9] like a doe . . . food *Orlando compares his own concern for the weakness of old age with another natural impulse, the concern of a mother for the weakness of her young.*

And know some nurture. But forbear, I say!
He dies that touches any of this fruit
Till I and my affairs are answerèd.

JAQUES   An you will not be answered with reason, I 100
must die.

DUKE SENIOR   What would you have? Your gentleness
shall force,
More than your force move us to gentleness.

ORLANDO   I almost die for food, and let me have it!

DUKE SENIOR   Sit down and feed, and welcome to our
table.

ORLANDO   Speak you so gently? Pardon me, I pray you,
I thought that all things had been savage here,
And therefore put I on the countenance
Of stern commandment. But whate'er you are
That in this desert inaccessible,   110
Under the shade of melancholy boughs,
Lose and neglect the creeping hours of time:
If ever you have looked on better days,
If ever been where bells have knolled to church,
If ever sat at any good man's feast,
If ever from your eyelids wiped a tear,
And know what 'tis to pity and be pitied,
Let gentleness my strong enforcement be;
In the which hope I blush, and hide my sword.

DUKE SENIOR   True is it that we have seen better days, 120
And have with holy bell been knolled to church,
And sat at good men's feasts, and wiped our eyes
Of drops that sacred pity hath engendered:
And therefore sit you down in gentleness,
And take upon command what help we have
That to your wanting may be ministered.

ORLANDO   Then but forbear your food a little while,
Whiles, like a doe, I go to find my fawn
And give it food. There is an old poor man
Who after me hath many a weary step   130
Limped in pure love. Till he be first sufficed,

[132] weak evils *evils causing weakness*

[133] find him out *find him*
[134] waste *consume*

[136] all alone *the only people to be*
[137] wide . . . theatre *Comparison between the theatre and the world at large was commonplace, but the Duke's reference to it gives Jaques his cue to develop the idea in his own characteristic way in the famous speech which follows.*
[138] pageants *scenes*

[144] Mewling *Crying; perhaps 'making sounds like a mewing cat'*

[148] woeful *full of woe (another mocking reference to the exaggerated follies of love)*
[149] Made to *Dedicated to*
[150] pard *leopard*
[151] Jealous in honour *Quick to take offence in questions of honour*
   sudden *impulsive*
[152] bubble reputation *fame as ephemeral as a bubble*
[154] capon *chicken (perhaps a reference to the practice of offering capons as bribes)*
[156] wise . . . instances *wise sayings and commonplace examples*
   modern *meaning 'commonplace', not 'present-day'.*
[158] pantaloon *dotard; absurd old man*

[160] hose, well saved *breeches, carefully preserved*

[163] his sound *its sound*

    Oppressed with two weak evils, age and hunger,
    I will not touch a bit.
DUKE SENIOR   Go find him out,
    And we will nothing waste till you return.
ORLANDO   I thank ye, and be blessed for your good
         comfort!   [*Exit*
DUKE SENIOR   Thou seest we are not all alone unhappy:
    This wide and universal theatre
    Presents more woeful pageants than the scene
    Wherein we play in.
JAQUES   All the world's a stage,
    And all the men and women merely players;   140
    They have their exits and their entrances,
    And one man in his time plays many parts,
    His Acts being seven ages. At first, the infant,
    Mewling and puking in the nurse's arms.
    Then the whining schoolboy, with his satchel
    And shining morning face, creeping like snail
    Unwillingly to school. And then the lover,
    Sighing like furnace, with a woeful ballad
    Made to his mistress' eyebrow. Then a soldier,
    Full of strange oaths and bearded like the pard, 150
    Jealous in honour, sudden and quick in quarrel,
    Seeking the bubble reputation
    Even in the cannon's mouth. And then the
        justice,
    In fair round belly, with good capon lined,
    With eyes severe and beard of formal cut,
    Full of wise saws and modern instances;
    And so he plays his part. The sixth age shifts
    Into the lean and slippered pantaloon,
    With spectacles on nose and pouch on side;
    His youthful hose, well saved, a world too wide 160
    For his shrunk shank, and his big manly voice,
    Turning again toward childish treble, pipes
    And whistles in his sound. Last Scene of all,
    That ends this strange eventful history,

[165] mere oblivion *utter forgetfulness*
[166] Sans *Without*

[169] most for *especially for your kindness to*

[175] unkind *unnatural*

[179] rude *rough*
[180] Heigh-ho *Not necessarily wistful.*
[181] Most friendship . . . folly *Although the song presents a sad view of the social world when compared with the natural, its generalisations are balanced against the particular instances we have just seen – true friendships on the part of both Duke Senior and Orlando, true gratitude on the part of Orlando and Adam. And love, which is certainly depicted often enough as folly, is also celebrated in this play.*

[187] warp *contract; turn to ice*

Is second childishness and mere oblivion,
Sans teeth, sans eyes, sans taste, sans everything.

Enter ORLANDO *with* ADAM

DUKE SENIOR   Welcome. Set down your venerable
    burden
    And let him feed.
ORLANDO   I thank you most for him.
ADAM   So had you need.
    I scarce can speak to thank you for myself.   170
DUKE SENIOR   Welcome, fall to. I will not trouble you
    As yet to question you about your fortunes.
    Give us some music; and, good cousin, sing.
AMIENS [*Sings*]
       Blow, blow, thou winter wind,
       Thou art not so unkind
         As man's ingratitude:
       Thy tooth is not so keen,
       Because thou art not seen,
         Although thy breath be rude.
     Heigh-ho, sing heigh-ho, unto the green holly.   180
     Most friendship is feigning, most loving mere folly:
       Then, heigh-ho, the holly,
       This life is most jolly.

       Freeze, freeze, thou bitter sky
       That dost not bite so nigh
         As benefits forgot:
       Though thou the waters warp,
       Thy sting is not so sharp
         As friend remembered not.
     Heigh-ho, sing heigh-ho, unto the green holly.   190
     Most friendship is feigning, most loving mere folly:
       Then, heigh-ho, the holly,
       This life is most jolly.
DUKE SENIOR   If that you were the good Sir Rowland's
    son,

[196] effigies   *likeness (accented on the second syllable)*
[197] limned   *portrayed*

[199] residue of your fortune   *remainder of your history*

As you have whispered faithfully you were,
And as mine eye doth his effigies witness
Most truly limned and living in your face,
Be truly welcome hither. I am the Duke
That loved your father. The residue of your
   fortune
Go to my cave and tell me. Good old man,   200
Thou art right welcome as thy master is.
Support him by the arm. Give me your hand,
And let me all your fortunes understand.
                               [*Exeunt*

ACT THREE, scene 1

Again we return briefly to the Court for a connecting episode in which we see Oliver (who has wronged his brother Orlando) confronting Duke Frederick (who has wronged his brother Duke Senior). As a result Oliver now joins the play's company of homeless wanderers.

[2] the better part . . . mercy *mostly a merciful man*

[3] argument *subject (i.e. Orlando)*

[4] thou present *when you are here*

[5] Find out *Discover*

[6] Seek him . . . candle *Seek him by day and night. A reference to Luke 15.8, which tells of the woman searching for her lost silver.*

[7] turn *return*

[11] quit thee *acquit yourself*

mouth *testimony (namely, the words he utters)*

[13] my heart *my true feelings*

[15] More villain thou *Oliver has just expressed sentiments identical with the Duke's own!*

[16] of such a nature *appropriate*

[17] extent *valuation*

[18] expediently *hastily*

turn him going *send him packing*

ACT THREE, scene 2

The Forest, which in Act 2 was touched by winter, old age and pessimism, is now taken over by youth and spring. The theme of romantic love takes precedence over all else, and Rosalind, controlling the action under the protection of her disguise, becomes increasingly dominant. The scene is a sequence of conversations, each with its bearing on one or other of the play's main themes.

[1] Hang there *Orlando is now engaged in the traditional vandalism of a besotted lover, festooning the greenery with doggerel and carving his beloved's name on trees. On the bare and non-representational stage of the Elizabethan theatre much of this would be left to the imagination; the verses were no doubt hung on a pillar.*

ACT THREE

Scene 1. *Enter* DUKE FREDERICK, LORDS *and* OLIVER

DUKE FREDERICK   Not see him since? Sir, sir, that
     cannot be.
    But were I not the better part made mercy,
    I should not seek an absent argument
    Of my revenge, thou present. But look to it:
    Find out thy brother, wheresoe'er he is;
    Seek him with candle; bring him dead or living
    Within this twelvemonth, or turn thou no more
    To seek a living in our territory.
    Thy lands, and all things that thou dost call thine
    Worth seizure, do we seize into our hands   10
    Till thou canst quit thee by thy brother's mouth
    Of what we think against thee.
OLIVER   O that your Highness knew my heart in this!
    I never loved my brother in my life.
DUKE FREDERICK   More villain thou. Well, push him
     out of doors,
    And let my officers of such a nature
    Make an extent upon his house and lands.
    Do this expediently, and turn him going.
                         [Exeunt

Scene 2. *Enter* ORLANDO

ORLANDO   Hang there, my verse, in witness of my love;
    And thou, thrice-crownèd Queen of Night,
     survey
    With thy chaste eye, from thy pale sphere above,
    Thy huntress' name that my full life doth sway.
    O Rosalind! These trees shall be my books,
    And in their barks my thoughts I'll character,
    That every eye which in this forest looks
    Shall see thy virtue witnessed everywhere.

[2] **thrice crowned ... Night** *Diana, goddess of chastity, was a triple goddess, being also Proserpina in the underworld and Luna (the moon) in the sky. Orlando also refers in these lines to three things associated with Diana: the moon, chastity, and hunting, and may be suggesting that she holds sway over all these.*

[4] **huntress** *Rosalind (who is chaste)*

    full *whole*

    sway *rule*

[6] **character** *write*

[10] **unexpressive** *inexpressible*

[13–21] **Truly, shepherd ... stomach** *Touchstone is not listing a series of opposites, but things which are totally or nearly identical. It is only his reported reactions which are opposites, designed to tease and bewilder Corin.*

  [15] **naught** *worthless*

  [16] **private** *secluded, cut off from the world*

  [19] **spare** *frugal*

    humour *disposition, mood*

  [21] **stomach** *(i) liking; (ii) physical appetite*

[23–31] **No more ... kindred** *Corin is not here a simple rustic producing laughable truisms. He is a shrewd old shepherd taking on Touchstone at his own game, and parading the obvious as rural wisdom.*

[25] **wants** *lacks*

[30] **complain of** *complain that he lacks. This remark, and the contrast of 'nature' and 'art' implies that neither he nor Touchstone has cause for such complaint.*

[30–1] **comes ... kindred** *descends from a very dull family*

[32] **natural philosopher** *a philosopher who observes nature closely. The compliment is made back-handed by the pun on 'natural', meaning 'fool'.*

[41] **manners** *A quibble. The first time it means 'polite behaviour', the second, 'moral character'.*

Run, run, Orlando, carve on every tree
The fair, the chaste, and unexpressive she.　　10
                                    [*Exit*

Enter CORIN *and* TOUCHSTONE

CORIN　And how like you this shepherd's life, Master
　Touchstone?
TOUCHSTONE　Truly, shepherd, in respect of itself, it is
　a good life; but in respect that it is a shepherd's life,
　it is naught. In respect that it is solitary, I like it very
　well; but in respect that it is private, it is a very vile
　life. Now in respect it is in the fields, it pleaseth me
　well; but in respect it is not in the court, it is tedious.
　As it is a spare life, look you, it fits my humour well;
　but as there is no more plenty in it, it goes much　　20
　against my stomach. Hast any philosophy in thee,
　shepherd?
CORIN　No more, but that I know the more one
　sickens, the worse at ease he is; and that he that
　wants money, means, and content is without three
　good friends; that the property of rain is to wet and
　fire to burn; that good pasture makes fat sheep; and
　that a great cause of the night is lack of the sun; that
　he that hath learned no wit by nature nor art may
　complain of good breeding, or comes of a very dull　　30
　kindred.
TOUCHSTONE　Such a one is a natural philosopher.
　Wast ever in court, shepherd?
CORIN　No, truly.
TOUCHSTONE　Then thou art damned.
CORIN　Nay, I hope.
TOUCHSTONE　Truly thou art damned, like an ill-
　roasted egg, all on one side.
CORIN　For not being at court? Your reason.
TOUCHSTONE　Why, if thou never wast at court, thou　　40
　never sawest good manners; if thou never sawest
　good manners, then thy manners must be wicked;

[44] parlous *perilous*

[45-8] Not a whit . . . court *This is not only sound sense, but a pertinent comment on the behaviour of some other characters. The incongruities of mixing court and country are sometimes the material of comedy, sometimes a way of affirming important values.*

[49] but you kiss *without kissing*
    but *unless*

[51] Instance *Give an example*

[52] still *constantly*

[53] fells *fleeces*

[54] your courtier's *any courtier's*

[55] mutton *sheep*

[63] civet *perfume (obtained from the 'flux', or gland, of the civet cat)*

[64] worms' meat *corpse; 'food for worms'*

[65] in respect of *in comparison with*

[66] perpend *consider*

[67-8] Mend the instance *Give a better example*

[71-2] God make incision . . . raw! *Either 'God cure your sickness by blood-letting' or 'God improve you by grafting, for you are a wild uncultivated plant'. Since the conversation is a contest between the wisdom of court and country, the second explanation is the more likely.*

[73-7] Sir, I am . . . lambs suck *This impressive little speech does not describe the idealised existence of the conventional shepherd in pastoral, but the fulfilled contentment of the countryman. We can approve its fine moral simplicities but also admire the ingenuity of Touchstone's repartee.*

[73] get *earn*

[75-6] content with my harm *patient under my sufferings*

[79] offer *dare*

and wickedness is sin, and sin is damnation. Thou
art in a parlous state, shepherd.

CORIN   Not a whit, Touchstone. Those that are good
manners at the court are as ridiculous in the country
as the behaviour of the country is most mockable at
the court. You told me you salute not at the court
but you kiss your hands. That courtesy would be
uncleanly if courtiers were shepherds.   50

TOUCHSTONE   Instance, briefly. Come, instance.

CORIN   Why, we are still handling our ewes, and their
fells you know are greasy.

TOUCHSTONE   Why, do not your courtier's hands
sweat? And is not the grease of a mutton as whole-
some as the sweat of a man? Shallow, shallow. A
better instance, I say. Come.

CORIN   Besides, our hands are hard.

TOUCHSTONE   Your lips will feel them the sooner.
Shallow again. A more sounder instance, come.   60

CORIN   And they are often tarred over with the surgery
of our sheep, and would you have us kiss tar? The
courtier's hands are perfumed with civet.

TOUCHSTONE   Most shallow man! Thou worms' meat
in respect of a good piece of flesh indeed! Learn of
the wise, and perpend. Civet is of a baser birth than
tar, the very uncleanly flux of a cat. Mend the instance, shepherd.

CORIN   You have too courtly a wit for me; I'll rest.

TOUCHSTONE   Wilt thou rest damned? God help thee,   70
shallow man! God make incision in thee, thou art
raw!

CORIN   Sir, I am a true labourer; I earn that I eat, get
that I wear, owe no man hate, envy no man's happiness, glad of other men's good, content with my
harm; and the greatest of my pride is to see my ewes
graze and my lambs suck.

TOUCHSTONE   That is another simple sin in you: to
bring the ewes and the rams together and to offer to

[81] bawd   *go-between, pander*
       bell-wether   *the leader of the flock, which carried a bell*
[82] cuckoldy   *A cuckold was a man whose wife was unfaithful to him, and references to such unfortunates provide an inexhaustible, but to the modern audience exhausting, supply of humour in Elizabethan drama.*

[83] out . . . match   *in unsuitable coupling*

[88] western Ind   *West Indies*

[92] lined *drawn*
[93] to   *compared with*

[98] the right . . . market   *just the jog-trot of butter-women on their way to market*

[100] taste   *example*

[101–12] If a hart . . . and Rosalind   *Touchstone's burlesque of the romantic verses is full of bawdy and insulting suggestions.*

[103] after kind   *seek its own species*

[105] lined   *Touchstone picks up 'lined' meaning 'drawn' from the verse that Rosalind read, and plays on two further senses of the word — to 'line' winter garments with extra cloth, and to 'line' meaning 'copulate', as a stallion copulates with, or 'covers' a mare.*
[107–8] They that reap . . . with Rosalind   *People must pay the penalty for what they have done. Rosalind must pay the price of her indecency by being whipped at the cart's tail like a prostitute.*

get your living by the copulation of cattle; to be   80
bawd to a bell-wether, and to betray a she-lamb of a
twelve-month to a crooked-pated old cuckoldly
ram, out of all reasonable match. If thou beest not
damned for this, the devil himself will have no shepherds; I cannot see else how thou shouldst 'scape.

CORIN Here comes young Master Ganymede, my
new mistress' brother.

Enter ROSALIND, *reading a paper*

ROSALIND [*Reads*]
       From the east to western Ind,
       No jewel is like Rosalind.
       Her worth, being mounted on the wind,   90
       Through all the world bears Rosalind.
       All the pictures fairest lined
       Are but black to Rosalind.
       Let no face be kept in mind
       But the fair of Rosalind.

TOUCHSTONE I'll rhyme you so eight years together,
dinners and suppers and sleeping hours excepted.
It is the right butterwomen's rank to market.

ROSALIND Out, fool!

TOUCHSTONE For a taste: 100
       If a hart do lack a hind,
       Let him seek out Rosalind.
       If the cat will after kind,
       So be sure will Rosalind.
       Wintered garments must be lined,
       So must slender Rosalind.
       They that reap must sheaf and bind,
       Then to cart with Rosalind.
       Sweetest nut hath sourest rind,
       Such a nut is Rosalind.   110
       He that sweetest rose will find
       Must find love's prick, and Rosalind.

[117] graff *graft*

[118] medlar *a kind of apple only fit to be eaten when overripe. Rosalind is punning on 'meddler'.*

[118-19] Then . . . country *then the fruit will be rotten earlier in the season*

[120] right virtue *proper quality*

[125] desert *desolate place*

[126] For *Merely because*

[130] erring *wandering*

[131] span *width of the stretched hand from tip of thumb to tip of little finger*

[132] Buckles in *Encloses*
      sum of age *span of life*

[139] The quintessence . . . sprite *The purest form of every spirit. The 'quintessence' was the fifth essence, additional to the four elements, of which in ancient philosophy the heavenly bodies were thought to be made.*

[140] in little *in the small world of mankind*

[141] Heaven Nature charged *Heaven instructed Nature*

[143] wide-enlarged *dispersed among a number of people*

[144] presently *at once*

[145] Helen's cheek *the facial beauty of Helen of Troy*
      but not her heart *because Helen was faithless*

This is the very false gallop of verses. Why do you
infect yourself with them?

ROSALIND   Peace, you dull fool! I found them on a tree.

TOUCHSTONE   Truly the tree yields bad fruit.

ROSALIND   I'll graff it with you and then I shall graff
it with a medlar. Then it will be the earliest fruit i'
th' country: for you'll be rotten ere you be half ripe,
and that's the right virtue of the medlar.   120

TOUCHSTONE   You have said; but whether wisely or
no, let the forest judge.

Enter CELIA, *with a writing*

ROSALIND   Peace! Here comes my sister, reading;
stand aside.

CELIA   [*Reads*]

> *Why should this a desert be?*
>   *For it is unpeopled? No.*
> *Tongues I'll hang on every tree*
>   *That shall civil sayings show:*
> *Some, how brief the life of man*
>   *Runs his erring pilgrimage,*   130
> *That the stretching of a span*
>   *Buckles in his sum of age;*
> *Some, of violated vows*
>   *'Twixt the souls of friend and friend;*
> *But upon the fairest boughs,*
>   *Or at every sentence end,*
> *Will I 'Rosalinda' write,*
>   *Teaching all that read to know –*
> *The quintessence of every sprite*
>   *Heaven would in little show.*   140
> *Therefore Heaven Nature charged*
>   *That one body should be filled*
> *With all graces wide-enlarged;*
>   *Nature presently distilled*
> *Helen's cheek, but not her heart,*
>   *Cleopatra's majesty,*

[147] **better part** *'physical skill' (as a runner); or perhaps 'determination to preserve her chastity'*

[148] **Sad . . . modesty** *Lucretia committed suicide after being raped by Tarquin.*

    Sad *Serious*

[149] **of** *from*

[150] **synod** *council*

[152] **touches . . . prized** *most highly valued traits*

[153] **would** *wished*

[155] **pulpiter** *preacher*

[158] **How now . . . friends.** *Celia is getting rid of Corin and Touchstone so that she can enjoy unrestricted teasing conversation with Rosalind.*

[161] **bag and baggage** *all our belongings (playing on 'baggage' meaning 'whore', which was Rosalind's nature in Touchstone's indecent poem)*

[162] **scrip and scrippage** *wallet and its contents*

[165–71] **feet . . . verse** *Rosalind and Celia play on 'feet' in verse, and 'feet' which support the body, and on 'bear' meaning 'endure' and 'carry'.*

[169] **lame** *(i) crippled; (ii) clumsy, inexpert*

[170] **without** *(i) unaided by; (ii) outside*

[173] **should be** *came to be*

[174–5] **seven . . . wonder** *Playing on the proverbial 'nine days' wonder', Rosalind says that she has already had time to get used to it.*

[176–8] **I was never . . . hardly remember** *An allusion (i) to the doctrine of Pythagoras that souls were transmitted from one animal to another and (ii) to the Irish belief that rats could be killed by rhyming spells.*

[179] **Trow you . . .?** *Do you know . . .?*

[181–2] **a chain . . . neck** *This remark alone makes it quite obvious who the lover is. Rosalind pursues the matter partly from a desire for incontestable certainty, and partly for the pleasure of behaving like a woman, which is only possible because Celia is in the secret.*

> *Atalanta's better part,*
> *Sad Lucretia's modesty.*
> *Thus Rosalind of many parts*
> *By heavenly synod was devised,* 150
> *Of many faces, eyes, and hearts,*
> *To have the touches dearest prized.*
> *Heaven would that she these gifts should have,*
> *An! I to live and die her slave.*

ROSALIND O most gentle pulpiter, what tedious homily of love have you wearied your parishioners withal, and never cried, 'Have patience, good people!'

CELIA How now? Back, friends. Shepherd, go off a little. Go with him, sirrah.

TOUCHSTONE Come, shepherd, let us make an honour- 160 able retreat; though not with bag and baggage, yet with scrip and scrippage.

[*Exit* TOUCHSTONE, *with* CORIN

CELIA Didst thou hear these verses?

ROSALIND O, yes, I heard them all, and more too; for some of them had in them more feet than the verses would bear.

CELIA That's no matter. The feet might bear the verses.

ROSALIND Ay, but the feet were lame, and could not bear themselves without the verse, and therefore 170 stood lamely in the verse.

CELIA But didst thou hear without wondering how thy name should be hanged and carved upon these trees?

ROSALIND I was seven of the nine days out of the wonder before you came; for look here what I found on a palm tree. I was never so be-rhymed since Pythagoras' time that I was an Irish rat, which I can hardly remember.

CELIA Trow you who hath done this?

ROSALIND Is it a man? 180

CELIA And a chain that you once wore, about his neck! Change you colour?

[184–5] friends to meet   *either Celia and Rosalind, or 'friends' meaning 'lovers', i.e. Rosalind and Orlando*

[188] Is it possible?   *Is it possible that you don't know?*

[193] out . . . whooping!   *more extraordinary than astonished cries can express*

[194] Good my complexion!   *Pardon my blushes*

[195] caparisoned   *dressed*

[195–6] I have . . . disposition   *my character is like a man's*

[197] a South Sea of discovery   *as long and drawn out as a voyage of exploration in the South Seas*

[198] apace   *quickly*

[199–200] this concealed man   *i.e. his name*

[204] So you may . . . belly   *copulate and conceive a child. Celia's frankness offsets Rosalind's mock-ornate style.*

[210] stay   *wait for*

[215] sad . . . maid   *with a serious face and on your maiden honour*

[219–24] Alas . . . one word   *Having prolonged the business of revelation to the maximum enjoyment of both girls, Rosalind now issues a series of breathless questions – partly serious (she really wants to know), partly play-acting (the impatient girl in love is an amusing role to parody).*

ROSALIND I prithee, who?

CELIA O Lord, Lord, it is a hard matter for friends to
meet; but mountains may be removed with earth-
quakes, and so encounter.

ROSALIND Nay, but who is it?

CELIA Is it possible?

ROSALIND Nay, I prithee now with most petitionary
vehemence, tell me who it is.   190

CELIA O wonderful, wonderful, and most wonderful,
wonderful, and yet again wonderful, and after that,
out of all whooping!

ROSALIND Good my complexion! Dost thou think,
though I am caparisoned like a man, I have a doublet
and hose in my disposition? One inch of delay more
is a South Sea of discovery. I prithee tell me who is
it quickly, and speak apace. I would thou couldst
stammer, that thou mightst pour this concealed
man out of thy mouth as wine comes out of a narrow-   200
mouthed bottle: either too much at once, or none at
all. I prithee take the cork out of thy mouth, that I
may drink thy tidings.

CELIA So you may put a man in your belly.

ROSALIND Is he of God's making? What manner of
man? Is his head worth a hat? Or his chin worth a
beard?

CELIA Nay, he hath but a little beard.

ROSALIND Why, God will send more, if the man will
be thankful. Let me stay the growth of his beard, if   210
thou delay me not the knowledge of his chin.

CELIA It is young Orlando, that tripped up the
wrestler's heels and your heart both in an instant.

ROSALIND Nay, but the devil take mocking! Speak
sad brow and true maid.

CELIA I' faith, coz, 'tis he.

ROSALIND Orlando?

CELIA Orlando.

ROSALIND Alas the day! What shall I do with my

[221–2] Wherein went he? *How was he dressed?*
[222] makes he *is he doing*

[225] Gargantua's mouth *a giant's mouth*

[227] more *a bigger problem*

[232] atomies *specks of dust*
[232–3] resolve the propositions of *find answers to the problems of*
[233] taste *description*
[234] relish . . . observance *put sauce on it by listening carefully*
[236] Jove's tree *The oak was sacred to Jove.*

[238] audience *hearing*

[240–1] like . . . knight *Celia, in mock-romantic mood, plays on chivalric language.*

[243] becomes . . . ground *embellishes the earth*
[244] 'holla' *stop*
    curvets *frisks around*
[245] furnished *dressed*
[246] heart *a pun on 'hart' (deer)*
[247] burden *refrain, or accompaniment*

[249–50] Do you not . . . speak *Again Rosalind indicates the pleasure of reverting to her feminine role, one characteristic of which is the inability to listen without interrupting. She exaggerates the trait in her enjoyment, which is partly caused by the fact that only Celia and the absent Touchstone do 'know she is a woman'. To behave like this affords relief as well as pleasure.*
[251] bring me out *put me off*

doublet and hose? What did he when thou sawest 220
him? What said he? How looked he? Wherein went
he? What makes he here? Did he ask for me? Where
remains he? How parted he with thee? And when
shalt thou see him again? Answer me in one word.

CELIA   You must borrow me Gargantua's mouth first;
'tis a word too great for any mouth of this age's size.
To say 'ay' and 'no' to these particulars is more
than to answer in a catechism.

ROSALIND   But doth he know that I am in this forest,
and in man's apparel? Looks he as freshly as he did 230
the day he wrestled?

CELIA   It is as easy to count atomies as to resolve the
propositions of a lover; but take a taste of my finding
him, and relish it with good observance. I found
him under a tree, like a dropped acorn.

ROSALIND   It may well be called Jove's tree when it
drops such fruit.

CELIA   Give me audience, good madam.

ROSALIND   Proceed.

CELIA   There lay he, stretched along like a wounded 240
knight.

ROSALIND   Though it be pity to see such a sight, it
well becomes the ground.

CELIA   Cry 'holla' to the tongue, I prithee; it curvets
unseasonably. He was furnished like a hunter.

ROSALIND   O, ominous! He comes to kill my heart.

CELIA   I would sing my song without a burden. Thou
bringest me out of tune.

ROSALIND   Do you not know I am a woman? When I
think, I must speak. Sweet, say on.   250

Enter ORLANDO *and* JAQUES

CELIA   You bring me out. Soft. Comes he not here?

ROSALIND   'Tis he! Slink by, and note him.

CELIA *and* ROSALIND *stand aside*

113

[254] had as lief   *would just as soon. Orlando and Jaques exchange polite courtesies which in fact are elaborately anti-social on both sides.*

[257] God buy you   *God be with you (the origin of 'goodbye')*

[258] better strangers   *the deliberate opposite of 'better friends'*

[262] ill-favouredly   *badly, or disapprovingly*

[264] just   *exactly so*

[271–2] conned . . . rings   *learned your pretty answers by heart, from the mottoes inscribed on rings*

[273–4] right . . . cloth   *with the brevity of texts (the equivalent of captions) inscribed on decorative painted scenes*

[276] Atalanta's heels   *an allusion to Atalanta's speed as a runner*

[279] breather   *living man*

[282] change   *exchange*

[284] By my troth   *By my faith*
        a fool   *i.e. Touchstone. Jaques implies, 'I sought one and found another'.*

[288] mine own figure   *my own face. It is not like Jaques to fall for that one!*

[289] cipher   *the figure O*

JAQUES I thank you for your company; but, good
faith, I had as lief have been myself alone.

ORLANDO And so had I; but yet, for fashion sake, I
thank you too for your society.

JAQUES God buy you; let's meet as little as we can.

ORLANDO I do desire we may be better strangers.

JAQUES I pray you mar no more trees with writing
love songs in their barks.   260

ORLANDO I pray you mar no more of my verses with
reading them ill-favouredly.

JAQUES Rosalind is your love's name?

ORLANDO Yes, just.

JAQUES I do not like her name.

ORLANDO There was no thought of pleasing you when
she was christened.

JAQUES What stature is she of?

ORLANDO Just as high as my heart.

JAQUES You are full of pretty answers. Have you not 270
been acquainted with goldsmiths' wives, and conned
them out of rings?

ORLANDO Not so; but I answer you right painted
cloth, from whence you have studied your questions.

JAQUES You have a nimble wit; I think 'twas made of
Atalanta's heels. Will you sit down with me, and we
two will rail against our mistress the world and all
our misery.

ORLANDO I will chide no breather in the world but
myself, against whom I know most faults.   280

JAQUES The worst fault you have is to be in love.

ORLANDO 'Tis a fault I will not change for your best
virtue. I am weary of you.

JAQUES By my troth, I was seeking for a fool when I
found you.

ORLANDO He is drowned in the brook. Look but in
and you shall see him.

JAQUES There I shall see mine own figure.

ORLANDO Which I take to be either a fool or a cipher.

[291–3] Love . . . Melancholy   *Orlando and Jaques confront each other as representatives of opposite types of folly, and as they part, each salutes what he finds most ridiculous in the other.*

[295] under that habit   *in that guise. 'Habit' also means 'dress', and Rosalind now resumes her manly pretence in an encounter full of ironic comedy.*

[297] What would you?   *What do you want?*

[304–5] Had not . . . proper?   *Wouldn't that have been just as appropriate?*

[306] divers   *various*

[307–8] who . . . withal   *with whom*

[311] trots hard   *trots at an uncomfortable pace*

[313] se'nnight   *a week*

[320] lean and wasteful   *causing one to go thin and waste away*

[325] go as softly   *walk as slowly*

JAQUES   I'll tarry no longer with you. Farewell, good 290
Signior Love.

ORLANDO   I am glad of your departure. Adieu, good
Monsieur Melancholy.   [*Exit* JAQUES

ROSALIND   [*to* CELIA] I will speak to him like a saucy
lackey, and under that habit play the knave with
him. Do you hear, forester?

ORLANDO   Very well. What would you?

ROSALIND   I pray you, what is't o'clock?

ORLANDO   You should ask me what time o'day.
There's no clock in the forest.   300

ROSALIND   Then there is no true lover in the forest,
else sighing every minute and groaning every hour
would detect the lazy foot of Time as well as a clock.

ORLANDO   And why not the swift foot of Time? Had
not that been as proper?

ROSALIND   By no means, sir, Time travels in divers
paces with divers persons. I'll tell you who Time
ambles withal, who Time trots withal, who Time
gallops withal, and who he stands still withal.

ORLANDO   I prithee, who doth he trot withal?   310

ROSALIND   Marry, he trots hard with a young maid
between the contract of her marriage and the day it is
solemnized. If the interim be but a se'nnight, Time's
pace is so hard that it seems the length of seven year.

ORLANDO   Who ambles Time withal?

ROSALIND   With a priest that lacks Latin and a rich
man that hath not the gout; for the one sleeps easily
because he cannot study, and the other lives merrily
because he feels no pain; the one lacking the burden
of lean and wasteful learning, the other knowing no 320
burden of heavy tedious penury. These Time
ambles withal.

ORLANDO   Who doth he gallop withal?

ROSALIND   With a thief to the gallows; for though he
go as softly as foot can fall, he thinks himself too
soon there.

[327] stays *stands*

[333] skirts *outskirts*

[335] cony *rabbit*
[336] kindled *born*

[338] purchase *acquire*
       removed *secluded*
[340] religious *a member of a religious order*
[341] inland *cultured; frequenting civilised places*
[342] courtship *(i) court life; (ii) wooing*
[343] read *deliver*
[344] touched *tainted*
[345–6] taxed . . . withal *accused of*

[348] laid . . . charge of *charged with*
[349] none principal *no outstanding ones*

[351] his *its*

[354–5] No, I will not . . . sick *I will give my advice only to
those who need it (A reference to Matthew 9.12.)*
[356] abuses *misuses*

[358] forsooth *in truth*
[359] fancy-monger *dealer in love*

[361] quotidian *daily and recurring fever*
[362] love-shaked *shaken by the fever of love*

ORLANDO Who stays it still withal?

ROSALIND With lawyers in the vacation; for they sleep
between term and term, and then they perceive not
how Time moves.   330

ORLANDO Where dwell you, pretty youth?

ROSALIND With this shepherdess, my sister; here in
the skirts of the forest, like fringe upon a petticoat.

ORLANDO Are you native of this place?

ROSALIND As the cony that you see dwell where she
is kindled.

ORLANDO Your accent is something finer than you
could purchase in so removed a dwelling.

ROSALIND I have been told so of many. But indeed an
old religious uncle of mine taught me to speak, who   340
was in his youth an inland man; one that knew
courtship too well, for there he fell in love. I have
heard him read many lectures against it, and I thank
God I am not a woman, to be touched with so many
giddy offences as he hath generally taxed their
whole sex withal.

ORLANDO Can you remember any of the principal
evils that he laid to the charge of women?

ROSALIND There were none principal. They were all
like one another as halfpence are, every one fault   350
seeming monstrous till his fellow fault came to
match it.

ORLANDO I prithee recount some of them.

ROSALIND No, I will not cast away my physic but on
those that are sick. There is a man haunts the forest
that abuses our young plants with carving 'Rosalind'
on their barks, hangs odes upon hawthorns, and
elegies on brambles; all, forsooth, deifying the name
of Rosalind. If I could meet that fancy-monger, I
would give him some good counsel, for he seems to   360
have the quotidian of love upon him.

ORLANDO I am he that is so love-shaked. I pray you
tell me your remedy.

[364] **uncle's marks** *symptoms described by my uncle*

[366] **cage of rushes** *i.e. a weak prison from which it is easy to escape*

[368–9] **blue eye** *dark rings round the eyes*

[369] **unquestionable** *resisting talk or questioning*

[372–3] **simply . . . revenue** *indeed, the quantity of beard you have is small, like a younger brother's income*

[374] **unbanded** *without a hat-band*

[376] **careless desolation** *despair that stopped you from caring for your appearance*

[377] **point-device** *fastidiously careful*

[378] **as loving** *like one who loves*

[382–3] **Me . . . love believe it** *Rosalind now initiates the greatest comedy of her charade, in which – as Ganymede – she is able to parody the manners of women and the whims of lovers, and – as Rosalind – to enjoy the feminine pleasure of being courted by the man she loves. She is able to speak the truth as Rosalind, and simultaneously give what seems to be a bracingly objective male account of female tactics.*

[385] **still** *always*

[388] **admired** *wondered at*

[395] **merely a** *nothing but*

[396] **a dark . . . whip** *customary treatment for the insane in Elizabethan times*

[397] **so punished** *punished in this way*

[399–400] **profess . . . counsel** *claim the skill of curing lovers merely by advice*

ROSALIND There is none of my uncle's marks upon
you. He taught me how to know a man in love; in
which cage of rushes I am sure you are not prisoner.

ORLANDO What were his marks?

ROSALIND A lean cheek, which you have not; a blue
eye and sunken, which you have not; an unquestionable spirit, which you have not; a beard neglected, 370
which you have not – but I pardon you for that, for
simply your having in beard is a younger brother's
revenue. Then your hose should be ungartered,
your bonnet unbanded, your sleeve unbuttoned, your
shoe untied, and everything about you demonstrat-
ing a careless desolation. But you are no such man:
you are rather point-device in your accoutrements,
as loving yourself, than seeming the lover of any
other.

mocking
satire to the
extremity
of opinions
on romantic
love

ORLANDO Fair youth, I would I could make thee 380
believe I love.

ROSALIND Me believe it? You may as soon make her
that you love believe it, which I warrant she is apter
to do than to confess she does: that is one of the
points in the which women still give the lie to their
consciences. But in good sooth, are you he that hangs
the verses on the trees, wherein Rosalind is so
admired?

ORLANDO I swear to thee, youth, by the white hand
of Rosalind, I am that he, that unfortunate he. 390

ROSALIND But are you so much in love as your rhymes
speak?

ORLANDO Neither rhyme nor reason can express how
much.

ROSALIND Love is merely a madness, and, I tell you,
deserves as well a dark house and a whip as madmen
do; and the reason why they are not so punished
and cured is that the lunacy is so ordinary that the
whippers are in love too. Yet I profess curing it by
counsel. 400

121

[405] moonish   *changeable, like the moon*

[406] fantastical   *full of fancies*
apish   *affected*

[408–9] for every . . . anything   *adopting some signs of every emotion, none of them genuine*

[410] cattle . . . colour   *people of this sort*

[411] entertain   *receive kindly*
forswear   *refuse*

[412] that   *with the result that*

[413] drave   *drove*
humour   *mood, disposition*

[414] living   *real*
humour of madness   *crazy inclination*

[415] forswear   *renounce*

[416] merely   *utterly*

[418] liver   *The liver was thought to be the seat of the emotions.*

[419] spot   *blemish*

[420] would not be cured   *do not wish to be cured*

[421–3] I would cure . . . woo me   *Rosalind thus manages to escape the inconvenience of her own pretence – her disguise as Ganymede – by luring Orlando to pretence instead. She controls the situation completely.*

[427] by the way   *on the way*

ACT THREE, scene 3
Touchstone now joins in the series of courtship conversations in a scene which burlesques the romantic feeling that we see in others. His wooing of a simple-minded rustic wench provides a sharp, debunking contrast, especially as his feelings appear to be less than serious and he retains the Clown's detachment.

[1] apace   *quickly*

[2–3] the man   *i.e. the man of your choice*

[3] feature   *form*

ORLANDO   Did you ever cure any so?

ROSALIND   Yes, one, and in this manner. He was to imagine me his love, his mistress; and I set him every day to woo me. At which time would I, being but a moonish youth, grieve, be effeminate, changeable, longing and liking, proud, fantastical, apish, shallow, inconstant, full of tears, full of smiles, for every passion something, and for no passion truly anything, as boys and women are for the most part cattle of this colour; would now like him, 410 now loathe him; then entertain him, then forswear him; now weep for him, then spit at him; that I drave my suitor from his mad humour of love to a living humour of madness, which was, to forswear the full stream of the world and to live in a nook merely monastic. And thus I cured him; and this way will I take upon me to wash your liver as clean as a sound sheep's heart, that there shall not be one spot of love in't.

ORLANDO   I would not be cured, youth.   420

ROSALIND   I would cure you, if you would but call me Rosalind, and come every day to my cote and woo me.

ORLANDO   Now, by the faith of my love, I will. Tell me where it is.

ROSALIND   Go with me to it, and I'll show it you; and by the way you shall tell me where in the forest you live. Will you go?

ORLANDO   With all my heart, good youth.

ROSALIND   Nay, you must call me Rosalind. Come, 430 sister, will you go?   [*Exeunt*

Scene 3. *Enter* TOUCHSTONE *and* AUDREY, *followed by* JAQUES

TOUCHSTONE   Come apace, good Audrey. I will fetch up your goats, Audrey. And now, Audrey, am I the man yet? Doth my simple feature content you?

[4] warrant *protect*

[6–8] goats . . . Goths *A series of concise scholastic witticisms which, of course, go straight over Audrey's head: Touchstone derives pleasure from exhibiting unnoticed learning. 'Goats' and 'goths' is a pun; the original meaning of 'capricious' is 'goat-like', which in turn meant 'lustful'; 'honest' means 'pure', and is therefore an unsuitable description of Ovid, who wrote erotic poetry.*

[9] ill-inhabited *poorly housed*

[10] Jove . . . house *The hidden Jaques appreciates Touchstone's learned wit and matches it. He refers to the hospitality given to the disguised Jove and Mercury by an old couple, Baucis and Philemon, in their humble cottage.*

[12] seconded with *supported by*
          forward *precocious*

[14] a great . . . room *a heavy bill for fare in a small inn-room. This is usually taken as a reference to the death of Christopher Marlowe, the poet and dramatist, who had been killed a few years earlier in a brawl concerning a tavern bill.*

[16] honest *pure*

[18–19] truest . . . feigning *best poetry is the most inventive*

[19] given to *in the habit of writing*

[20–1] what they swear . . . feign *as lovers they do not perform what they promise to do in their poems. Touchstone is playing with words, especially 'feign' meaning (i) 'invent'; (ii) 'pretend', with a possible third play on 'fain' meaning 'desire'.*

[28] hard-favoured *ugly*

[30] honey . . . sugar *i.e. too much of a good thing*

[31] material *full of ideas*

[34–6] Truly . . . dish *Since Audrey sets store by 'honesty', Touchstone has now turned it into an unsuitable virtue for both the beautiful and the ugly.*

[38] foul *Audrey means only 'plain-featured', not 'ugly'.*

AUDREY Your features, Lord warrant us! What features?

TOUCHSTONE I am here with thee and thy goats, as the most capricious poet, honest Ovid, was among the Goths.

JAQUES [*Aside*] O knowledge ill-inhabited, worse than Jove in a thatched house! 10

TOUCHSTONE When a man's verses cannot be understood, nor a man's good wit seconded with the forward child, understanding, it strikes a man more dead than a great reckoning in a little room. Truly, I would the gods had made thee poetical.

AUDREY I do not know what 'poetical' is. Is it honest in deed and word? Is it a true thing?

TOUCHSTONE No, truly; for the truest poetry is the most feigning, and lovers are given to poetry, and what they swear in poetry may be said as lovers they 20 do feign.

AUDREY Do you wish then that the gods had made me poetical?

TOUCHSTONE I do, truly; for thou swearest to me thou art honest. Now, if thou wert a poet, I might have some hope thou didst feign.

AUDREY Would you not have me honest?

TOUCHSTONE No, truly, unless thou wert hard-favoured; for honesty coupled to beauty is to have honey a sauce to sugar. 30

JAQUES [*Aside*] A material fool.

AUDREY Well, I am not fair, and therefore I pray the gods make me honest.

TOUCHSTONE Truly, and to cast away honesty upon a foul slut were to put good meat into an unclean dish.

AUDREY I am not a slut, though I thank the gods I am foul.

TOUCHSTONE Well, praised be the gods for thy foulness! Sluttishness may come hereafter. But be it as 40

[44] couple *marry*

[45] fain *like to*

[48] stagger . . . attempt *waver in this enterprise*

[50] horn-beasts *A play on 'horned animals' and 'cuckolds' – i.e. deceived husbands who were reputed to wear horns on their foreheads.*

what though? *what does it matter?*

[51] necessary *unavoidable*

[51–3] Many a man . . . of them *Many men do not know the full extent of their possessions, and many men possess faithless wives without knowing it*

[54] dowry *what his wife brings him*

[55] Poor men alone? *Is it only poor men who have them?*

[56] rascal *poorer deer in the herd*

[60–2] defence . . . want *it is better to have the art of defensive swordsmanship than not to, and equally it is better to have a faithless wife than none at all*

[66] give *give in marriage*

[73–4] God 'ield you *God reward you*

[74] last company *latest companionship (i.e. at this present opportune moment)*

[75] Even a toy *Just a trivial matter*

pray be covered *put your hat back on. Jaques has removed his hat in deference to the priest and the solemn occasion, but Touchstone elects to regard it as an act of respect to himself.*

it may be, I will marry thee; and to that end I have
been with Sir Oliver Martext, the vicar of the next
village, who hath promised to meet me in this place
of the forest and to couple us.

JAQUES [*Aside*]   I would fain see this meeting.

AUDREY   Well, the gods give us joy!

TOUCHSTONE   Amen. A man may, if he were of a
fearful heart, stagger in this attempt; for here we
have no temple but the wood, no assembly but
horn-beasts. But what though? Courage! As horns   50
are odious, they are necessary. It is said, 'Many a
man knows no end of his goods.' Right! Many a man
has good horns and knows no end of them. Well,
that is the dowry of his wife; 'tis none of his own
getting. Horns? Even so. Poor men alone? No, no;
the noblest deer hath them as huge as the rascal. Is
the single man therefore blessed? No; as a walled
town is more worthier than a village, so is the forehead of a married man more honourable than the
bare brow of a bachelor; and by how much defence   60
is better than no skill, by so much is a horn more
precious than to want.

Enter SIR OLIVER MARTEXT

Here comes Sir Oliver. Sir Oliver Martext, you are
well met. Will you dispatch us here under this tree,
or shall we go with you to your chapel?

OLIVER MARTEXT   Is there none here to give the woman?

TOUCHSTONE   I will not take her on gift of any man.

OLIVER MARTEXT   Truly, she must be given, or the
marriage is not lawful.

JAQUES [*Comes forward*]   Proceed, proceed; I'll give   70
her.

TOUCHSTONE   Good even, good Master What-ye-call't.
How do you, sir? You are very well met. God 'ield
you for your last company; I am very glad to see you.
Even a toy in hand here, sir. Nay, pray be covered.

[76] motley *fool*
[77] bow *yoke*

[79] desires *So Touchstone equates men's desires with various forms of animal servitude.*

bill *caress each other with their bills (hence 'billing and cooing' as a derogatory term for courtship)*

[85] wainscot *wooden panelling*
[86] green *unseasoned*

[88] not ... mind but *inclined to think that*
[89] of another *by another clergyman*
[90] like *likely*

[95] in bawdry *in sin*

[104] fantastical *wittily imaginative. Sir Oliver, left deserted by this merry departure, tries to repair his dignity.*

ACT THREE, scene 4

Once again we see Rosalind alone with Celia, and therefore able to drop her masculine pretence. As Ganymede she is the scorner of love, as Rosalind she is its victim, and we see here the depth of her feeling for Orlando. Celia, as always an admirable foil to Rosalind's pretence, takes up the mocking function which Rosalind has momentarily put aside, and directs it at Rosalind herself. With Corin's appearance, an artificial love-convention is introduced in contrast to Rosalind's genuine depth of feeling.

[3] tears ... man *a swift pointer to the mood of the scene. Rosalind's tempestuous feminine mood is not to escape teasing. Celia refuses to take 'weeping' seriously.*

JAQUES Will you be married, motley?

TOUCHSTONE As the ox hath his bow, sir, the horse his curb, and the falcon her bells, so man hath his desires; and as pigeons bill, so wedlock would be nibbling.   80

JAQUES And will you, being a man of your breeding, be married under a bush like a beggar? Get you to church, and have a good priest that can tell you what marriage is. This fellow will but join you together as they join wainscot; then one of you will prove a shrunk panel and, like green timber, warp, warp.

TOUCHSTONE [*Aside*] I am not in the mind but I were better to be married of him than of another; for he is not like to marry me well; and not being well married, it will be a good excuse for me hereafter to leave my wife.   90

JAQUES Go thou with me and let me counsel thee.

TOUCHSTONE Come, sweet Audrey.
We must be married, or we must live in bawdry.
Farewell, good Master Oliver; not

> O sweet Oliver,
> O brave Oliver,
> Leave me not behind thee;

but   100

> Wind away,
> Be gone, I say;
> I will not to wedding with thee.

OLIVER MARTEXT 'Tis no matter. Ne'er a fantastical knave of them all shall flout me out of my calling.

[*Exeunt*

Scene 4. *Enter* ROSALIND *and* CELIA

ROSALIND Never talk to me; I will weep.

CELIA Do, I prithee; but yet have the grace to consider that tears do not become a man.

[7] dissembling colour *deceitful colour, i.e. red: traditionally the colour of Judas' hair*

[9] Judas' . . . children *i.e. they are deceitful. When Celia appears to confirm Rosalind's suspicions of Orlando, Rosalind at once springs to his defence. With this, too, Celia mockingly agrees.*

[11] Your chestnut *Chestnut*

[14] holy bread *sacramental bread*

[15] cast . . . Diana *lips cast for a statue of Diana, goddess of chastity*

[16] of winter's sisterhood *of total chastity*

[24] concave *hollow*

[30] tapster *inn-waiter, who would reckon up the bill*

[31] confirmers . . . reckonings *testify to false statements*

[33-7] I met . . . Orlando *Rosalind is briefly diverted by Celia's red herring – long enough to record another example of her spirited masculine pretence, and to remind us of the Duke, who has not been on stage for some time.*

[34] question *talk*

[38] brave *fine. Celia is ironical at Rosalind's expense.*

[38-42] He . . . swears . . . goose *Orlando's romantic oaths glance crosswise off his loved one's heart, instead of thrusting straight at it; just as, in tilting, an inexperienced competitor, spurring his horse on one side only, breaks his lance with a glancing blow.*

ROSALIND But have I not cause to weep?

CELIA As good cause as one would desire; therefore weep.

ROSALIND His very hair is of the dissembling colour.

CELIA Something browner than Judas'. Marry, his kisses are Judas' own children.

ROSALIND I' faith, his hair is of a good colour. 10

CELIA An excellent colour. Your chestnut was ever the only colour.

ROSALIND And his kissing is as full of sanctity as the touch of holy bread.

CELIA He hath bought a pair of cast lips of Diana. A nun of winter's sisterhood kisses not more religiously; the very ice of chastity is in them.

ROSALIND But why did he swear he would come this morning, and comes not?

CELIA Nay, certainly there is no truth in him. 20

ROSALIND Do you think so?

CELIA Yes; I think he is not a pickpurse nor a horse-stealer, but for his verity in love, I do think him as concave as a covered goblet or a worm-eaten nut.

ROSALIND Not true in love?

CELIA Yes, when he is in, but I think he is not in.

ROSALIND You have heard him swear downright he was.

CELIA 'Was' is not 'is'. Besides, the oath of a lover is no stronger than the word of a tapster; they are both 30 the confirmers of false reckonings. He attends here in the forest on the Duke your father.

ROSALIND I met the Duke yesterday and had much question with him. He asked me of what parentage I was. I told him, of as good as he; so he laughed and let me go. But what talk we of fathers when there is such a man as Orlando?

CELIA O, that's a brave man! He writes brave verses, speaks brave words, swears brave oaths, and breaks them bravely, quite traverse, athwart the heart of 40

[42–3] But all's brave . . . guides   *Another explicit linking of the grandeur and the folly of love.*

[46–8] shepherd . . . shepherdess   *With these conventional figures we are brought back to the world of pastoral artifice, in which love is a game of exaggerated adoration and scorn.*

[46] complained of   *lamented about*

[50] pageant   *The word suggests something deliberately theatrical, inviting the presence of spectators. Rosalind, recovering her spirits with her masculine role, proposes (with more truth than she knows) to be an active participant rather than a watcher.*

[54] mark   *observe*
     remove   *move away*

ACT THREE, scene 5
The love-dialogue of Silvius and Phebe adds pastoral convention to the 'types' of love we are seeing, which have recently included Orlando and Rosalind, and Touchstone and Audrey. Rosalind, again in her controlling male disguise, intervenes to correct the extremity of Phebe's wounding discourtesy, and so precipitates a further comic development.

[5] Falls   *Lets fall*
[6] But first begs   *Without first asking*
[7] dies and lives   *gains his whole living*

[8–27] I would not . . . hurt   *The whole speech is a taunting*

his lover, as a puisny tilter, that spurs his horse but
on one side, breaks his staff like a noble goose. But
all's brave that youth mounts and folly guides. Who
comes here?

Enter CORIN

CORIN　Mistress and master, you have oft enquired
　　　After the shepherd that complained of love,
　　　Who you saw sitting by me on the turf,
　　　Praising the proud disdainful shepherdess
　　　That was his mistress.
CELIA　　　　　　　　Well, and what of him?
CORIN　If you will see a pageant truly played　　　　　50
　　　Between the pale complexion of true love
　　　And the red glow of scorn and proud disdain,
　　　Go hence a little, and I shall conduct you,
　　　If you will mark it.
ROSALIND　　　　　　O, come, let us remove:
　　　The sight of lovers feedeth those in love.
　　　Bring us to this sight, and you shall say
　　　I'll prove a busy actor in their play.
　　　　　　　　　　　　　　　　　　[Exeunt

Scene 5. *Enter* SILVIUS *and* PHEBE

SILVIUS　Sweet Phebe, do not scorn me; do not, Phebe!
　　　Say that you love me not, but say not so
　　　In bitterness. The common executioner,
　　　Whose heart th' accustomed sight of death
　　　　makes hard,
　　　Falls not the axe upon the humbled neck
　　　But first begs pardon. Will you sterner be
　　　Than he that dies and lives by bloody drops?

Enter ROSALIND, CELIA *and* CORIN, *unnoticed*

PHEBE　I would not be thy executioner.
　　　I fly thee, for I would not injure thee.

denunciation of the romantic cliché that the loved one's eyes have power to kill. It does, of course, truthfully expose an absurd exaggeration, but such truthful cruelty is perilous in those who, like Phebe, mistakenly suppose themselves immune. In contrast, Rosalind's power to expose the follies of love derives its impressiveness from our knowledge of her own predicament.

[8] would not   *do not wish to be*

[11] sure   *surely*

[13] atomies   *motes of dust*

[17] swound   *swoon*

[19] Lie not, to say   *Do not tell lies by saying*

[21] but   *merely*

[23] cicatrice . . . impressure   *mark and observable impression*

[28] as that . . . near   *an anticipatory irony shortly before Rosalind's entrance*

[29] fresh   *fresh-complexioned*
power of fancy   *power to arouse your love*

[36] Who . . . mother . . . ?   *i.e. Who do you think you are?*

[38] What though . . . ?   *What if . . . ?*

Thou tell'st me there is murder in mine eye: 10
'Tis pretty, sure, and very probable
That eyes, that are the frail'st and softest things,
Who shut their coward gates on atomies,
Should be called tyrants, butchers, murderers.
Now I do frown on thee with all my heart,
And if mine eyes can wound, now let them kill
   thee.
Now counterfeit to swound; why, now fall down;
Or if thou canst not, O, for shame, for shame,
Lie not, to say mine eyes are murderers.
Now show the wound mine eye hath made in
   thee.   20
Scratch thee but with a pin, and there remains
Some scar of it; lean upon a rush,
The cicatrice and capable impressure
Thy palm some moment keeps; but now mine
   eyes,
Which I have darted at thee, hurt thee not,
Nor, I am sure, there is no force in eyes
That can do hurt.

SILVIUS   O dear Phebe,
If ever – as that ever may be near –
You meet in some fresh cheek the power of
   fancy,
Then shall you know the wounds invisible   30
That love's keen arrows make.

PHEBE   But till that time
Come not thou near me; and when that time
   comes,
Afflict me with thy mocks, pity me not,
As till that time I shall not pity thee.

ROSALIND [*coming forward*]   And why, I pray you?
   Who might be your mother,
That you insult, exult, and all at once,
Over the wretched? What though you have no
   beauty

[39–40] I see . . . bed   *I do not see in you so much beauty as would light up a darkened bedroom without the aid of a candle. Rosalind scoffs at another romantic exaggeration.*

[43–4] ordinary . . . sale-work   *usual run of nature's ready-made goods*

[44] 'Od's   *May God save*

[45] tangle   *entangle*

[47] bugle   *black, bead-like*

[48] to your worship   *to worship you*

[50] south   *south wind*

[51] properer   *more handsome*

[53] ill-favoured   *foolish*

[55] out of you   *in your image of her*

proper   *handsome*

[61] Cry . . . mercy   *Ask the man for forgiveness*

[62] Foul . . . scoffer   *The worst kind of ugliness is a combination of physical ugliness and contempt*

[70] sauce   *rebuke. Note Rosalind's prompt, brisk assessment of the situation.*

[73] in wine   *under the influence of drink*

ACT THREE, SCENE FIVE

(As, by my faith, I see no more in you
Than without candle may go dark to bed)
Must you be therefore proud and pitiless?   40
Why, what means this? Why do you look on me?
I see no more in you than in the ordinary
Of nature's sale-work. 'Od's my little life,
I think she means to tangle my eyes too!
No, faith, proud mistress, hope not after it;
'Tis not your inky brows, your black silk hair,
Your bugle eyeballs, nor your cheek of cream
That can entame my spirits to your worship.
You foolish shepherd, wherefore do you follow
      her,
Like foggy south, puffing with wind and rain?   50
You are a thousand times a properer man
Than she a woman. 'Tis such fools as you
That makes the world full of ill-favoured children.
'Tis not her glass, but you, that flatters her,
And out of you she sees herself more proper
Than any of her lineaments can show her.
But mistress, know yourself. Down on your knees,
And thank heaven, fasting, for a good man's love!
For I must tell you friendly in your ear,
Sell when you can, you are not for all markets.   60
Cry the man mercy, love him, take his offer;
Foul is most foul, being foul to be a scoffer;
So take her to thee, shepherd. Fare you well.

PHEBE   Sweet youth, I pray you chide a year together;
      I had rather hear you chide than this man woo.

ROSALIND [Aside]   He's fallen in love with your foulness,
      and she'll fall in love with my anger. If it be so, as
      fast as she answers thee with frowning looks,
      I'll sauce her with bitter words.
            [to Phebe]   Why look you so upon me?   70

PHEBE   For no ill will I bear you.

ROSALIND   I pray you do not fall in love with me,
      For I am falser than vows made in wine.

137

[75] hard by   *near*

[78–9] Though all the world . . . he   *If everyone in the world could see you, none except Silvius could be so deceived as to think you beautiful*

[80] to our flock   *A reminder that Rosalind and Celia too are shepherds (in their temporary disguise) just as Silvius and Phebe are (in an idealised pastoral form) and as others, such as Corin, really are.*

[81] Dead shepherd   *The 'pastoral' shepherd mourned here is Marlowe, from whose poem* Hero and Leander *the following line is taken. This elegiac pastoral term is a tribute to the dead poet. As a conventional pastoral figure Phebe is an appropriate person to speak these lines.*

   saw   *maxim*

[89] extermined   *destroyed*

[91] that were   *that would be*

[93] yet it is not   *even now it is not true*

[95] erst   *before*
[96] employ   *i.e. she will give him tasks, which the devoted lover in pastoral should gladly perform for his mistress.*

[100] in such . . . grace   *having received so little graciousness from you*

[103] That . . . reaps   *Who gathers the main harvest of your love*

[104] scattered   *random*

Besides, I like you not. If you will know my
    house,
'Tis at the tuft of olives, here hard by.
Will you go, sister? Shepherd, ply her hard.
Come, sister. Shepherdess, look on him better,
And be not proud. Though all the world could
    see,
None could be so abused in sight as he.
Come, to our flock.   80

              [*Exit* ROSALIND *with* CELIA *and* CORIN

PHEBE   Dead shepherd, now I find thy saw of might,
    'Who ever loved that loved not at first sight?'
SILVIUS   Sweet Phebe.
PHEBE   Ha! What say'st thou, Silvius?
SILVIUS   Sweet Phebe, pity me.
PHEBE   Why, I am sorry for thee, gentle Silvius.
SILVIUS   Wherever sorrow is, relief would be.
    If you do sorrow at my grief in love,
    By giving love your sorrow and my grief
    Were both extermined.
PHEBE   Thou hast my love. Is not that neighbourly?   90
SILVIUS   I would have you.
PHEBE   Why, that were covetousness.
    Silvius, the time was that I hated thee;
    And yet it is not that I bear thee love,
    But since that thou canst talk of love so well,
    Thy company, which erst was irksome to me,
    I will endure; and I'll employ thee too;
    But do not look for further recompense
    Than thine own gladness that thou art employed.
SILVIUS   So holy and so perfect is my love,
    And I in such a poverty of grace,   100
    That I shall think it a most plenteous crop
    To glean the broken ears after the man
    That the main harvest reaps. Loose now and
        then
    A scattered smile, and that I'll live upon.

[107] bounds *lands*
[108] carlot *churl, peasant*
[109–19] Think not . . . And yet 'tis well *This series of fluctu-
ating opinions is an exaggerated version of the unstable views we saw
Rosalind expressing about the missing Orlando in the last scene. It is
part of the play's diagnosis of love's characteristic follies.*

[114] becomes *befits*

[123] damask *colour of damask roses*

[125] In parcels *Feature by feature*
[125–6] gone . . . fall *come close to falling*

[129] what . . . do *what business was it of his*

[131] am remembered *remember*
[132] answered not again *did not answer back*
[133] all one *no matter*
      omittance . . . quittance *omitting to do something at the
time does not remove the chance or duty to make up for it later*

PHEBE   Know'st thou the youth that spoke to me
      erewhile?

SILVIUS   Not very well, but I have met him oft,
      And he hath bought the cottage and the bounds
      That the old carlot once was master of.

PHEBE   Think not I love him, though I ask for him;
      'Tis but a peevish boy; yet he talks well.   110
      But what care I for words? Yet words do well
      When he that speaks them pleases those that
        hear.
      It is a pretty youth. Not very pretty.
      But sure he's proud. And yet his pride becomes
        him.
      He'll make a proper man. The best thing in him
      Is his complexion. And faster than his tongue
      Did make offence, his eye did heal it up.
      He is not very tall. Yet for his years he's tall.
      His leg is but so so. And yet 'tis well.
      There was a pretty redness in his lip,
      A little riper and more lusty red   120
      Than that mixed in his cheek. 'Twas just the
        difference
      Betwixt the constant red and mingled damask.
      There be some women, Silvius, had they
        marked him
      In parcels, as I did, would have gone near
      To fall in love with him; but for my part,
      I love him not, nor hate him not. And yet
      I have more cause to hate him than to love him;
      For what had he to do to chide at me?
      He said mine eyes were black and my hair   130
        black;
      And, now I am remembered, scorned at me.
      I marvel why I answered not again.
      But that's all one: omittance is no quittance.
      I'll write to him a very taunting letter.
      And thou shalt bear it. Wilt thou, Silvius?

[136] straight   *immediately*

[138] passing short   *very abrupt*

SILVIUS Phebe, with all my heart. *What a wimp...*

PHEBE   I'll write it straight;
The matter's in my head and in my heart;
I will be bitter with him and passing short.
Go with me, Silvius.

                                        [*Exeunt*

ACT FOUR, scene 1

After a preliminary exchange between Rosalind and Jaques,
which further clarifies Jaques' place in the play, we have the
main episode of wooing between Ganymede and Orlando
Both reveal their true feelings under cover of the make-believe,
and the scene is rich in comic ironies. Rosalind again uses her
vantage-point of pretence in order to 'misuse' her sex while
simultaneously enjoying the true feminine satisfactions of
concealed courtship. In this scene true and pretended feeling
become almost indistinguishable.

[3] melancholy fellow *Confronted with Rosalind, Jaques reveals*
his 'melancholy' (a neurotic state which was deeply interesting to the
audiences of this period) as the self-admiring affectation which it
actually is.

[5-7] in extremity . . . drunkards *Rosalind deplores excess, at*
both ends of the spectrum of behaviour. She stands for a sane moder-
ation which Jaques, with his extremes of mood and behaviour, seems
incapable of achieving. (But is he incapable of it?)

modern *commonplace*

[8] sad *serious*

[11] emulation *jealousy*
fantastical *fanciful*

[14] politic *crafty; decided by the dictates of policy*
nice *fastidious, finicky*

[16] simples *ingredients*

[18-19] my often rumination *my frequent meditation*

[19] humorous *moody*

[25] I have . . . experience *This remark, like the preceding speech,*
is more than a little self-congratulatory: its solemnity is self-conscious

[26-8] I had rather . . . sad *Jaques has been fascinated by*
Touchstone, and the play has developed an implicit contrast between
them: Jaques is the sad fool, Touchstone the merry fool. In effect
Rosalind, the central intelligence of the play, now makes her own
choice between the attitudes they represent.

ACT 4

JAQUES   I prithee, pretty youth, let me be better
acquainted with thee.

ROSALIND   They say you are a melancholy fellow.

JAQUES   I am so; I do love it better than laughing.

ROSALIND   Those that are in extremity of either are
abominable fellows, and betray themselves to every
modern censure worse than drunkards.

JAQUES   Why, 'tis good to be sad and say nothing.

ROSALIND   Why then, 'tis good to be a post.

JAQUES   I have neither the scholar's melancholy, which   10
is emulation; nor the musician's, which is fantastical; nor the courtier's, which is proud; nor the
soldier's, which is ambitious; nor the lawyer's,
which is politic; nor the lady's, which is nice; nor
the lover's, which is all these: but it is a melancholy
of mine own, compounded of many simples, ex-
tracted from many objects, and indeed the sundry
contemplation of my travels, in which my often
rumination wraps me in a most humorous sadness.

ROSALIND   A traveller! By my faith, you have great   20
reason to be sad. I fear you have sold your own
lands to see other men's. Then to have seen much
and to have nothing is to have rich eyes and poor
hands.

JAQUES   Yes, I have gained my experience.

Enter ORLANDO

ROSALIND   And your experience makes you sad. I had
rather have a fool to make me merry than experience
to make me sad – and to travel for it too!

ORLANDO   Good day and happiness, dear Rosalind.

[30] **God buy you** *God be with you. Jaques beats a hasty retrea[t]
at the abhorrent sight of a romantic lover.*

      an *if*

[32–7] **Farewell ... gondola** *Rosalind cites some frequent com[-]
plaints against the affectations of travellers.*

[33] **lisp** *put on a foreign accent*

      disable *belittle*

[36–7] **swam in a gondola** *i.e. been in Venice*

[38] **An** *If*

[40–1] **within ... promise** *under an hour late. We have alread[y]
seen the effect on Rosalind of this brief delay.*

[46] **clapped ... shoulder** *arrested*

      warrant *guarantee*

[49] **an** *if*

[53] **jointure** *marriage-settlement*

[57] **horns** *i.e. the horns of a cuckold*

[58] **beholding** *indebted*

[59] **armed ... fortune** *already equipped with what he wi[ll]
acquire later in any case, as a result of his marriage*

      prevents the slander *anticipates the disgrace (not th[e]
modern sense of 'prevents')*

[65] **leer** *complexion (not 'cunning smile')*

JAQUES   Nay then, God buy you, an you talk in blank 30
verse.   [*Exit*

ROSALIND   Farewell, Monsieur Traveller. Look you
lisp and wear strange suits, disable all the benefits of
your own country, be out of love with your nativity,
and almost chide God for making you that countenance you are; or I will scarce think you have swam in
a gondola. Why, how now, Orlando, where have you
been all this while? You a lover? An you serve me
such another trick, never come in my sight more.

ORLANDO   My fair Rosalind, I come within an hour of 40
my promise.

ROSALIND   Break an hour's promise in love? He that
will divide a minute into a thousand parts and break
but a part of the thousandth part of a minute in the
affairs of love, it may be said of him that Cupid hath
clapped him o' th' shoulder, but I'll warrant him
heart-whole.

ORLANDO   Pardon me, dear Rosalind.

ROSALIND   Nay, an you be so tardy, come no more in
my sight. I had as lief be wooed of a snail.   50

ORLANDO   Of a snail?

ROSALIND   Ay, of a snail; for though he comes slowly,
he carries his house on his head: a better jointure, I
think, than you make a woman. Besides, he brings
his destiny with him.

ORLANDO   What's that?

ROSALIND   Why, horns; which such as you are fain to
to be beholding to your wives for; but he comes
armed in his fortune and prevents the slander of his
wife.   60

ORLANDO   Virtue is no horn-maker, and my Rosalind
is virtuous.

ROSALIND   And I am your Rosalind.

CELIA   It pleases him to call you so; but he hath a
Rosalind of a better leer than you.

ROSALIND   Come, woo me, woo me; for now I am in

[67] humour *mood*
   like *likely*

[68] an *if*

[72] gravelled *stuck (grounded, like a ship on the sand)*

[74] out *at a loss for words*

[74–5] God warn us! *God warrant us! i.e. is it likely that th*
could happen?

[75] shift *expedient*

[78] matter *material for conversation*

[79] out *at a loss for words*

[82–3] I should think . . . wit *I should think my virtue stronge*
than my wits (if I couldn't put a stop to your talk)

[84] suit *courtship. Rosalind, in her reply, puns on 'sui*
meaning 'courtship' and 'clothes'.

[87–8] I take . . . of her *Ironically, Orlando acknowledges h*
deliberate pretence that he is talking to Rosalind, while the repl
to her question is a perfectly straightforward 'yes'.

[91] Then . . . die *Orlando now begins the kind of romant*
exaggeration which we saw in the previous scene, when Phebe attacke
such sentiments in Silvius.

[92] by attorney *by proxy. Rosalind mocks Orlando's protes*
ation with a legal quibble – 'authorise someone else to die for yo
rather than perform the deed yourself'.

[95] videlicet *namely (another legal term)*

[95–106] Troilus . . . not for love *Rosalind scoffs at the suppose*
lethal qualities of unrequited love by reference to love-martyrs c
classical legend. The speech is deflating, as Phebe's was to Silviu.
Yet its effect is quite different: it is not only devoid of intentional malic
but closes with an elegiac'tone which recognises the destructive powe
of time. Lovers die, even if it is not love that kills them.

[95–6] Troilus . . . Grecian club *There are several accounts c*
how Troilus, son of Priam the King of Troy, and lover of the faithles
Cressida, actually met his death. Rosalind appears to select this or
for its totally unromantic nature.

[96–7] he did . . . before *an ironic criticism of the 'true lover's*
suicidal inclinations

[97] patterns *ideals*

[98] Leander *Supposedly he swam the Hellespont each nigh*
to meet Hero at Sestos, and drowned. Rosalind finds a deflating
everyday reason for this sad event.

[103] it was . . . Sestos *Hero of Sestos was the cause of his death*

a holiday humour and like enough to consent. What
would you say to me now, an I were your very, very
Rosalind?

ORLANDO   I would kiss before I spoke.   70

ROSALIND   Nay, you were better speak first, and when
you were gravelled for lack of matter, you might
take occasion to kiss. Very good orators, when they
are out, they will spit; and for lovers lacking – God
warn us! – matter, the cleanliest shift is to kiss.

ORLANDO   How if the kiss be denied?

ROSALIND   Then she puts you to entreaty, and there
begins new matter.

ORLANDO   Who could be out, being before his beloved
mistress?   80

ROSALIND   Marry, that should you, if I were your
mistress, or I should think my honesty ranker than
my wit.

ORLANDO   What, of my suit?

ROSALIND   Not out of your apparel, and yet out of your
suit. Am not I your Rosalind?

ORLANDO   I take some joy to say you are, because I
would be talking of her.

ROSALIND   Well, in her person, I say I will not have
you.   90

ORLANDO   Then, in mine own person, I die.

ROSALIND   No, faith, die by attorney. The poor world
is almost six thousand years old, and in all this time
there was not any man died in his own person,
videlicet, in a love cause. Troilus had his brains
dashed out with a Grecian club; yet he did what he
could to die before, and he is one of the patterns of
love. Leander, he would have lived many a fair year
though Hero had turned nun, if it had not been for
a hot midsummer night: for, good youth, he went 100
but forth to wash him in the Hellespont, and being
taken with the cramp, was drowned; and the foolish
chroniclers of that age found it was 'Hero of Sestos'.

[107] right   *true*

[107–8] of this mind   *holding this view*

[108] her frown . . . kill me   *more romantic hyperbole, recalling Phebe's scornful answer to Silvius: 'Thou tell'st me there is murder in mine eye'.*

[111] coming-on   *encouraging*

[122–3] you shall . . . marry us   *another mock-wedding, following the proceedings of Touchstone and Audrey. But underlying the superficial pretence is, as the audience knows, an exchange of vows which is true on both sides.*

[136] commission   *authority (to take 'her' as wife)*

[138] goes before   *anticipates. As Ganymede, she has not waited for Celia to ask her; as Rosalind, she has not waited for the true ceremony.*

[138–9] a woman's thought   *Rosalind now prepares the way for some generalisations at the expense of womanhood.*

But these are all lies. Men have died from time to
time, and worms have eaten them, but not for
love.

ORLANDO I would not have my right Rosalind of this
mind, for I protest her frown might kill me.

ROSALIND By this hand, it will not kill a fly. But
come, now I will be your Rosalind in a more 110
coming-on disposition; and ask me what you will,
I will grant it.

ORLANDO Then love me, Rosalind.

ROSALIND Yes, faith, will I, Fridays and Saturdays
and all.

ORLANDO And wilt thou have me?

ROSALIND Ay, and twenty such.

ORLANDO What sayest thou?

ROSALIND Are you not good?

ORLANDO I hope so. 120

ROSALIND Why then, can one desire too much of a
good thing? Come, sister, you shall be the priest and
marry us. Give me your hand, Orlando. What do
you say, sister?

ORLANDO Pray thee marry us.

CELIA I cannot say the words.

ROSALIND You must begin, 'Will you, Orlando—'

CELIA Go to. Will you, Orlando, have to wife this
Rosalind?

ORLANDO I will. 130

ROSALIND Ay, but when?

ORLANDO Why, now, as fast as she can marry us.

ROSALIND Then you must say, 'I take thee, Rosalind,
for wife.'

ORLANDO I take thee, Rosalind, for wife.

ROSALIND I might ask you for your commission; but
I do take thee, Orlando, for my husband. There's a
girl goes before the priest, and certainly a woman's
thought runs before her actions.

ORLANDO So do all thoughts; they are winged. 140

[150] against *anticipating*
      newfangled *distracted by novelties*
[151] giddy *unstable*
[152] Diana . . . fountain *a statue of Diana in the centre of a fountain*
[154] hyen *hyena*

[156] she will . . . do *Again Rosalind is able to speak the exact truth, and at the same time elaborate the pretence.*

[159] Make *Close*

[164] whither wilt? *where are you going?*

[170] Marry *By the Virgin Mary*
[171] take *catch*

[173] her husband's occasion *a chance to find fault with her husband*

ROSALIND Now tell me how long you would have her
after you have possessed her.

ORLANDO For ever and a day.

ROSALIND Say 'a day,' without the 'ever'. No, no,
Orlando. Men are April when they woo, December
when they wed. Maids are May when they are
maids, but the sky changes when they are wives. I
will be more jealous of thee than a Barbary cock-
pigeon over his hen, more clamorous than a parrot
against rain, more newfangled than an ape, more 150
giddy in my desires than a monkey. I will weep for
nothing, like Diana in the fountain, and I will do
that when you are disposed to be merry; I will laugh
like a hyen, and that when thou art inclined to sleep.

ORLANDO But will my Rosalind do so?

ROSALIND By my life, she will do as I do.

ORLANDO O, but she is wise.

ROSALIND Or else she could not have the wit to do
this; the wiser, the waywarder. Make the doors
upon a woman's wit, and it will out at the casement; 160
shut that, and 'twill out at the keyhole; stop that,
'twill fly with the smoke out at the chimney.

ORLANDO A man that had a wife with such a wit, he
might say, 'Wit, whither wilt?'

ROSALIND Nay, you might keep that check for it till
you met your wife's wit going to your neighbour's
bed.

ORLANDO And what wit could wit have to excuse
that?

ROSALIND Marry, to say she came to seek you there. 170
You shall never take her without her answer, unless
you take her without her tongue. O, that woman
that cannot make her fault her husband's occasion,
let her never nurse her child herself, for she will
breed it like a fool.

ORLANDO For these two hours, Rosalind, I will leave
thee.

[178–9] Alas . . . hours! *Orlando has announced his departure abruptly, and Rosalind's dismayed reply, which can of course be passed off as more play-acting, is genuine. She recovers quickly, and in her next speech is again able to parody a lover's distress as well as feel it.*

[185] but one . . . away *only one woman cast off*

[192] pathetical *emotion-stirring*

[194] gross *(i) total; (ii) large*

[197] no less . . . than *just as religiously as*

[200] try *judge*

[201] simply misused *utterly disgraced*
        love-prate *lover's ranting*
[205–8] O coz . . . Portugal *Again Rosalind reverts to her womanly role the moment she is alone with Celia, and enjoys the relief of expressing her feelings without concealment.*
[207] sounded *measured, like the depth of water*
[209] bottomless *With this joke Celia again tries to play for Rosalind the role that Rosalind plays for others – poking amiable fun at extremes of feeling.*
[211] bastard . . . Venus *Cupid, blind son of Venus, begotten not by her husband Vulcan but by Mercury*
[212] thought *fancy*
        spleen *capricious impulse*
[213] abuses *deceives*

ROSALIND Alas, dear love, I cannot lack thee two hours!

ORLANDO I must attend the Duke at dinner. By two 180 o'clock I will be with thee again.

ROSALIND Ay, go your ways, go your ways: I knew what you would prove. My friends told me as much, and I thought no less. That flattering tongue of yours won me. 'Tis but one cast away, and so, come death! Two o'clock is your hour?

ORLANDO Ay, sweet Rosalind.

ROSALIND By my troth, and in good earnest, and so God mend me, and by all pretty oaths that are not dangerous, if you break one jot of your promise, or 190 come one minute behind your hour, I will think you the most pathetical break-promise, and the most hollow lover, and the most unworthy of her you call Rosalind, that may be chosen out of the gross band of the unfaithful. Therefore beware my censure and keep your promise.

ORLANDO With no less religion than if thou wert indeed my Rosalind. So, adieu.

ROSALIND Well, Time is the old justice that examines all such offenders, and let Time try. Adieu!   200

[*Exit* ORLANDO

CELIA You have simply misused our sex in your love-prate. We must have your doublet and hose plucked over your head, and show the world what the bird hath done to her own nest.

ROSALIND O coz, coz, coz, my pretty little coz, that thou didst know how many fathom deep I am in love! But it cannot be sounded: my affection hath an unknown bottom, like the Bay of Portugal.

CELIA Or rather, bottomless, that as fast as you pour affection in, it runs out.   210

ROSALIND No, that same wicked bastard of Venus that was begot of thought, conceived of spleen, and born of madness, that blind rascally boy that abuses every

[215] Aliena *Rosalind's rare use of Celia's assumed name is a sign that she is desperately clinging to her own assumed role.*

[216–17] find . . . come *It is now Rosalind's turn to behave like a conventional distressed lover, in contrast with Celia's down-to-earth plan for a quick nap.*

ACT FOUR, scene 2
The main function of this brief scene is to mark the passage of time between Scenes 1 and 3, but it also serves as a reminder of Duke Senior and his companions. The physical duress of forest life prescribes its own festivals, one of which is the celebration of successful hunting.

[5] branch of victory *i.e. like the laurels of a victor in battle*

[6] forester *There may be 'foresters' present as well as the lords, but it would be quite natural for Jaques to address one of the lords in this way, because of their dress.*

[8–9] 'Tis no matter . . . enough *This is the second time we have seen Jaques request music. He clearly takes more pleasure in it than he will admit.*

[14–19] Take thou . . . to scorn *The implication of the song is that all men must risk wearing a cuckold's horns.*

ACT FOUR, scene 3
The first part of this scene extends the complications which follow from Phebe's infatuation with Ganymede, and shows Rosalind again in her male guise as corrective manipulator. The second part introduces a reformed Oliver, and with his story, which almost overthrows Rosalind's masquerade, we begin to move towards a resolution of the play.

[2] much *ironical: there is no sign of him*

[4–5] he hath ta'en . . . sleep *he went out hunting and fell asleep instead*

156

one's eyes because his own are out, let him be judge
how deep I am in love. I'll tell thee, Aliena, I cannot
be out of the sight of Orlando. I'll go find a shadow,
and sigh till he come.

CELIA   And I'll sleep. [*Exeunt*

Scene 2. Enter JAQUES; *and* LORDS, *dressed as foresters*

JAQUES   Which is he that killed the deer?

LORD   Sir, it was I.

JAQUES   Let's present him to the Duke like a Roman
conqueror; and it would do well to set the deer's
horns upon his head for a branch of victory. Have
you no song, forester, for this purpose?

ANOTHER LORD   Yes, sir.

JAQUES   Sing it. 'Tis no matter how it be in tune, so it
make noise enough.

[*Music*

SONG

What shall he have that killed the deer?   10
His leather skin and horns to wear:
 Then sing him home. The rest shall bear
 This burden.

Take thou no scorn to wear the horn,
It was a crest ere thou wast born,
 Thy father's father wore it,
 And thy father bore it.
The horn, the horn, the lusty horn,
Is not a thing to laugh to scorn.

[*Exeunt*

Scene 3. Enter ROSALIND *and* CELIA

ROSALIND   How say you now, is it not past two o'clock?
And here much Orlando!

CELIA   I warrant you, with pure love and troubled
brain, he hath ta'en his bow and arrows and is gone
forth to sleep.

[12] tenor   *tone, import*

[13] but as   *merely*

[14] startle at   *be startled by*

[15] play the swaggerer   *act like one provoked*
　　　Bear . . . all!   *If one could bear this, one could bear any-thing!*

[18] phoenix   *a legendary bird. Only one could be alive at once, as the new bird was born from the ashes of its single ancestor.*
　　　'Od's my will!   *As God's will is my will!*

[21] device   *invention*

[24] turned into   *brought to*

[25–30] I saw . . . his hand   *In this speech and what follows, Rosalind, as Ganymede, pours the utmost possible scorn on the absent Phebe. Her objective is to help Silvius to win his loved one, and to chasten her beforehand. These speeches should be seen as a carefully judged mixture of provocation, reassurance and encourage-ment for Silvius, not as a wanton assault on Phebe.*

[26] freestone   *tawny brown in colour*

[28] housewife's   *i.e. rough and coarse*

[30] hand   *handwriting (not 'hand' as in the preceding lines)*

[35] giant-rude   *excessively barbaric*

[36] Ethiop   *Ethiopian, therefore black, therefore evil and threatening*

Enter SILVIUS

Look who comes here.

SILVIUS   My errand is to you, fair youth.
My gentle Phebe did bid me give you this.
                    Gives ROSALIND *a letter*
I know not the contents, but as I guess
By the stern brow and waspish action   10
Which she did use as she was writing of it,
It bears an angry tenor. Pardon me;
I am but as a guiltless messenger.

ROSALIND   Patience herself would startle at this letter
And play the swaggerer. Bear this, bear all!
She says I am not fair, that I lack manners;
She calls me proud, and that she could not love
    me,
Were man as rare as phoenix. 'Od's my will!
Her love is not the hare that I do hunt!
Why writes she so to me? Well, shepherd, well,   20
This is a letter of your own device.

SILVIUS   No, I protest, I know not the contents.
Phebe did write it.

ROSALIND   Come, come, you are a fool,
And turned into the extremity of love.
I saw her hand. She has a leathern hand,
A freestone-coloured hand. I verily did think
That her old gloves were on, but 'twas her
    hands.
She has a housewife's hand; but that's no matter.
I say she never did invent this letter;
This is a man's invention and his hand.   30

SILVIUS   Sure it is hers.

ROSALIND   Why, 'tis a boisterous and a cruel style,
A style for challengers. Why, she defies me
Like Turk to Christian. Women's gentle brain
Could not drop forth such giant-rude invention,
Such Ethiop words, blacker in their effect

159

[37] countenance   *appearance (black with ink)*

[39] too much   *i.e. too much already*

[40] Phebes me   *writes to me in her own style*

[41] god, to shepherd   *Phebe's address to Rosalind maintains the pastoral conventions to which she and Silvius belong.*

[45] laid apart   *put on one side for a time*

[48–64] Whiles . . . how to die   *Phebe now invokes the principal love-excesses that she and Rosalind, in their different ways, have mocked: she talks of the hurtful power of the loved one's eyes, and the fatal, or suicidal, effects of thwarted love.*

[49] vengeance   *harm*

[50] Meaning . . . beast   *Rosalind chooses to take Phebe's lines as accusing her of being a beast, whereas Phebe means that she is a god.*

[51] eyne   *eyes*

[54] in mild aspect   *by looking favourably. This is probably an astrological reference to the beneficial or harmful position in the sky of those heavenly bodies, Rosalind's eyes.*

[59] seal . . . mind   *send a sealed message containing your answer*

[60] kind   *disposition*

[62] make   *either 'bring as a dowry' or 'do'*

[69] instrument   *(i) tool; (ii) musical instrument, on which she plays 'false strains'*

[71] tame snake   *a poor creature, deprived of your power to poison*

Than in their countenance. Will you hear the
 letter?

SILVIUS So please you, for I never heard it yet;
 Yet heard too much of Phebe's cruelty.

ROSALIND She Phebes me. Mark how the tyrant writes. 40
[*Reads*] *Art thou god, to shepherd turned*
   That a maiden's heart hath burned?
Can a woman rail thus?

SILVIUS Call you this railing?

ROSALIND [*Reads*]
   Why, thy godhead laid apart,
   Warr'st thou with a woman's heart?
Did you ever hear such railing?
   Whiles the eye of man did woo me,
   That could do no vengeance to me.
Meaning me a beast.   50
   If the scorn of your bright eyne
   Have power to raise such love in mine,
   Alack, in me what strange effect
   Would they work in mild aspect!
   Whiles you chid me, I did love;
   How then might your prayers move?
   He that brings this love to thee
   Little knows this love in me;
   And by him seal up thy mind,
   Whether that thy youth and kind 60
   Will the faithful offer take
   Of me and all that I can make,
   Or else by him my love deny,
   And then I'll study how to die.

SILVIUS Call you this chiding?

CELIA Alas, poor shepherd!

ROSALIND Do you pity him? No, he deserves no pity.
Wilt thou love such a woman? What, to make thee
an instrument and play false strains upon thee? Not
to be endured! Well, go your way to her, for I see 70
love hath made thee a tame snake, and say this to

[77] purlieus *fringes*

[79] neighbour bottom *next valley*

[80] rank *row*
[81] Left *Passed by*

[84] If that . . . tongue *If I can recognise you from what I have been told*

[87] favour *complexion*
[87-8] bestows . . . sister *has the manner of a mature (or older) sister (of Celia)*
[88] low *short*

[92] commend him *send his compliments*

[94] napkin *handkerchief*

[96] know of *learn from*

[102] sweet . . . fancy *'sweet' because of his pretence with Ganymede; 'bitter' because of his continued separation from Rosalind*
fancy *love*

her: that if she love me, I charge her to love thee;
if she will not, I will never have her unless thou
entreat for her. If you be a true lover, hence, and not
a word; for here comes more company.

[*Exit* SILVIUS

Enter OLIVER

OLIVER   Good morrow, fair ones. Pray you, if you
    know,
    Where in the purlieus of this forest stands
    A sheepcote, fenced about with olive trees?
CELIA   West of this place, down in the neighbour
    bottom.
    The rank of osiers by the murmuring stream   80
    Left on your right hand brings you to the place.
    But at this hour the house doth keep itself;
    There's none within.
OLIVER   If that an eye may profit by a tongue,
    Then should I know you by description.
    Such garments and such years: 'The boy is fair,
    Of female favour, and bestows himself
    Like a ripe sister; the woman low,
    And browner than her brother.' Are not you
    The owner of the house I did enquire for?   90
CELIA   It is no boast, being asked, to say we are.
OLIVER   Orlando doth commend him to you both,
    And to that youth he calls his 'Rosalind'
    He sends this bloody napkin. Are you he?
ROSALIND   I am. What must we understand by this?
OLIVER   Some of my shame, if you will know of me
    What man I am, and how and why and where
    This handkercher was stained.
CELIA   I pray you tell it.
OLIVER   When last the young Orlando parted from you,
    He left a promise to return again   100
    Within an hour; and pacing through the forest,
    Chewing the food of sweet and bitter fancy,

163

[103] threw his eye *glanced*

[110] nimble in threats *weaving threateningly*

[113] indented *zigzag*

[115] drawn dry *sucked dry by her cubs*

[117] When that *Waiting until*

[119] as dead *as if it were dead*

[123] render him *describe him as*

[128] purposed so *intended to*
[129] kindness *(i) kinship; (ii) generosity*
[130] nature *natural feeling*
        just occasion *legitimate pretext (for abandoning Oliver to his fate)*
[132] hurtling *tumult*

Lo, what befell! He threw his eye aside,
And mark what object did present itself:
Under an oak, whose boughs were mossed with
    age
And high top bald with dry antiquity,
A wretched ragged man, o'ergrown with hair,
Lay sleeping on his back. About his neck
A green and gilded snake had wreathed itself,
Who, with her head nimble in threats,
    approached   110
The opening of his mouth; but suddenly,
Seeing Orlando, it unlinked itself
And with indented glides did slip away
Into a bush, under which bush's shade
A lioness, with udders all drawn dry,
Lay couching, head on ground, with catlike
    watch
When that the sleeping man should stir; for 'tis
The royal disposition of that beast
To prey on nothing that doth seem as dead.
This seen, Orlando did approach the man   120
And found it was his brother, his elder brother.

CELIA   O! I have heard him speak of that same brother,
And he did render him the most unnatural
That lived amongst men.

OLIVER   And well he might so do,
For well I know he was unnatural.

ROSALIND   But to Orlando: did he leave him there,
Food to the sucked and hungry lioness?

OLIVER   Twice did he turn his back and purposed so;
But kindness, nobler ever than revenge,
And nature, stronger than his just occasion,   130
Made him give battle to the lioness,
Who quickly fell before him; in which hurtling
From miserable slumber I awaked.

CELIA   Are you his brother?

ROSALIND   Was't you he rescued?

[135] contrive   *plot*

[136] 'Twas I . . . not I   *It was I as I was in my unconverted state, not I as I now am*

[138] being the thing   *now that I am the person*

[139] for . . . napkin?   *what about the bloody handkerchief? Rosalind's concern is solely for Orlando in this conversation, while Celia is already showing an interest in Oliver.*

[141] our recountments . . . bathed   *had washed the narratives of our adventures*

[142] As   *Such as*
    desert   *desolate*

[143] In brief   *But not very brief! How is Rosalind behaving during this speech?*

[144] entertainment   *hospitality*

[151] Brief   *In brief*
    recovered   *restored*

[152] small space   *short time*

[163-4] You a man . . . heart   *This is the first time that Rosalind has revealed her feminine nature to anyone not in the secret of her disguise. Having played the man so successfully, she now has to pretend that playing the woman is part of her performance for Orlando. She can still react with enough spirit to relish concealed truthfulness, in 'I do so, I confess it'.*

CELIA Was't you that did so oft contrive to kill him?

OLIVER 'Twas I. But 'tis not I. I do not shame
　　　To tell you what I was, since my conversion
　　　So sweetly tastes, being the thing I am.

ROSALIND But, for the bloody napkin?

OLIVER 　　　　　　　　By and by.
　　　When from the first to last, betwixt us two,　　140
　　　Tears our recountments had most kindly
　　　　　bathed,
　　　As how I came into that desert place:
　　　In brief, he led me to the gentle Duke,
　　　Who gave me fresh array and entertainment,
　　　Committing me unto my brother's love,
　　　Who led me instantly unto his cave,
　　　There stripped himself, and here upon his arm
　　　The lioness had torn some flesh away,
　　　Which all this while had bled; and now he
　　　　fainted,
　　　And cried, in fainting, upon Rosalind.　　150
　　　Brief, I recovered him, bound up his wound;
　　　And after some small space, being strong at
　　　　heart,
　　　He sent me hither, stranger as I am,
　　　To tell this story, that you might excuse
　　　His broken promise, and to give this napkin,
　　　Dyed in his blood, unto the shepherd youth
　　　That he in sport doth call his 'Rosalind'.

　　　　　　　ROSALIND *faints*

CELIA Why, how now, Ganymede, sweet Ganymede!

OLIVER Many will swoon when they do look on blood.

CELIA There is more in it. Cousin Ganymede!　　160

OLIVER Look, he recovers.

ROSALIND I would I were at home.

CELIA 　　　　　　We'll lead you thither.
　　　I pray you, will you take him by the arm?

OLIVER Be of good cheer, youth. You a man? You
lack a man's heart.

[167] counterfeited *imitated*

[169–70] passion of earnest *genuine emotion*

[174–5] So I do . . . right *More concealed truth-telling. Note how deftly the comic mode has been restored after the solemnity and tension of Oliver's narrative.*

[176] draw *withdraw*

ROSALIND   I do so, I confess it. Ah, sirrah, a body would think this was well counterfeited. I pray you tell your brother how well I counterfeited. Heigh-ho!

OLIVER   This was not counterfeit. There is too great testimony in your complexion that it was a passion of earnest.   170

ROSALIND   Counterfeit, I assure you.

OLIVER   Well then, take a good heart and counterfeit to be a man.

ROSALIND   So I do; but, i' faith, I should have been a woman by right.

CELIA   Come, you look paler and paler. Pray you draw homewards. Good sir, go with us.

OLIVER   That will I, for I must bear answer back
          How you excuse my brother, Rosalind.

ROSALIND   I shall devise something. But I pray you 180 commend my counterfeiting to him. Will you go?

                                        [*Exeunt*

ACT FIVE, scene 1

Love and marriage, the overriding concern of the rest of the play, are in the forefront from the beginning of Act 5, but absurdly so at first, in this comic love-quarrel over a country bumpkin between Touchstone, the professional intelligent fool and William, a fool to the manner born.

[8–9] no interest in me   *no claim to me*

[11] clown   *yokel*
[12] shall be flouting   *must jeer*
[13] hold   *restrain ourselves*
[14] even   *evening*
[15] God ye   *God give you*

[17–18] Cover thy head   *Put your hat on. For the second time Touchstone resorts to aristocratic condescension.*

ACT 5

Scene 1. *Enter* TOUCHSTONE *and* AUDREY

TOUCHSTONE We shall find a time, Audrey. Patience, gentle Audrey.

AUDREY Faith, the priest was good enough, for all the old gentleman's saying.

TOUCHSTONE A most wicked Sir Oliver, Audrey, a most vile Martext. But, Audrey, there is a youth here in the forest lays claim to you.

AUDREY Ay, I know who 'tis. He hath no interest in me in the world. Here comes the man you mean.

Enter WILLIAM

TOUCHSTONE It is meat and drink to me to see a   10
clown. By my troth, we that have good wits have much to answer for. We shall be flouting; we cannot hold.

WILLIAM Good even, Audrey.

AUDREY God ye good even, William.

WILLIAM And good even to you, sir.

TOUCHSTONE Good even, gentle friend. Cover thy head, cover thy head. Nay, prithee be covered. How old are you, friend?   *condescending*

WILLIAM Five-and-twenty, sir.   20

TOUCHSTONE A ripe age. Is thy name William?

WILLIAM William, sir.

TOUCHSTONE A fair name. Wast born i' th' forest here?

WILLIAM Ay, sir, I thank God.

TOUCHSTONE 'Thank God.' A good answer. Art rich?

WILLIAM Faith, sir, so so.

TOUCHSTONE 'So so' is good, very good, very excellent good; and yet it is not, it is but so so. Art thou wise?

WILLIAM Ay, sir, I have a pretty wit.   30

[33–7] The heathen . . . open   *This elaborate statement is probably a comment on William's appearance, as he stands open-mouthed with astonishment.*

[42] figure   *standard device. What follows is nonsense, intended to confuse William.*

[44] consent   *agree*

[45] ipse   *Latin for 'he himself'*

[48–9] in the vulgar   *in common language (likewise 'boorish' and 'common')*

[52–3] to thy better understanding   *to make it clearer for you*

[53] to wit   *that is to say*

[56] bastinado   *beating with a cudgel*
        in steel   *with a sword*

[56–7] bandy . . . faction   *exchange insults and disagreements with you*

[57] policy   *unprincipled scheming*

TOUCHSTONE Why, thou sayest well. I do now remember a saying: 'The fool doth think he is wise,
but the wise man knows himself to be a fool.' The
heathen philosopher, when he had a desire to eat a
grape, would open his lips when he put it into his
mouth, meaning thereby that grapes were made to
eat and lips to open. You do love this maid?

WILLIAM I do, sir.

TOUCHSTONE Give me your hand. Art thou learned?

WILLIAM No, sir.   40

TOUCHSTONE Then learn this of me: to have is to
have. For it is a figure in rhetoric that drink, being
poured out of a cup into a glass, by filling the one
doth empty the other; for all your writers do consent
that *ipse* is he. Now, you are not *ipse*, for I am he.

WILLIAM Which he, sir?

TOUCHSTONE He, sir, that must marry this woman.
Therefore, you clown, abandon – which is in the
vulgar, leave – the society – which in the boorish is,
company – of this female – which in the common is,   50
woman. Which together is, abandon the society of
this female, or, clown, thou perishest; or, to thy
better understanding, diest; or, to wit, I kill thee,
make thee away, translate thy life into death, thy
liberty into bondage. I will deal in poison with thee,
or in bastinado, or in steel; I will bandy with thee
in faction; I will o'errun thee with policy; I will kill
thee a hundred and fifty ways. Therefore tremble
and depart.

AUDREY Do, good William.   60

WILLIAM God rest you merry, sir.   [*Exit*

Enter CORIN

CORIN Our master and mistress seek you. Come
away, away!

TOUCHSTONE Trip, Audrey, trip, Audrey. I attend,
I attend.   [*Exeunt*

ACT FIVE, scene 2

With the revelation of Oliver's sudden and reciprocated love for Celia, and further arrangements for the future of another four lovers, the action moves some distance forward in this scene towards the forthcoming revelations and marital unions of the play's ending. The meeting arranged by Rosalind is clearly to mark the solution of all complications.

[1–3] **Is't possible . . . love her?** *In a play where love at first sight is the rule, and Orlando himself a victim of it, it is ironical that he should ask this question with such apparent surprise. In Act 1 it was Celia, now a partner in this latest precipitate love-match, who asked Rosalind an identical question.*

[5] **giddiness** *rashness*

[12] **estate** *settle*

live . . . shepherd *It is a further mark of Oliver's reform that, like the others, he is now willing to accept the pleasures and privations of a shepherd's life.*

[14] **all's** *all his*

[18] **fair sister** *Oliver accepts the pretence that Ganymede is Rosalind; it is not necessary to suppose that he is suggesting awareness of her true sex.*

[24] **Wounded . . . lady** *Orlando accepts the cue provided by Rosalind, and resumes his romantic exaggeration.*

[29] **where you are** *what you are referring to*

[31] **thrasonical** *boastful (in the style of the bragging soldier Thraso, in Terence's play* Eunuch)

Scene 2. *Enter* ORLANDO *and* OLIVER

ORLANDO   Is't possible that on so little acquaintance you should like her? That, but seeing, you should love her? And loving, woo? And wooing, she should grant? And will you persever to enjoy her?

OLIVER   Neither call the giddiness of it in question, the poverty of her, the small acquaintance, my sudden wooing, nor her sudden consenting; but say with me, 'I love Aliena'; say with her that she loves me; consent with both that we may enjoy each other. It shall be to your good, for my father's house, 10 and all the revenue that was old Sir Rowland's, will I estate upon you, and here live and die a shepherd.

Enter ROSALIND

ORLANDO   You have my consent. Let your wedding be tomorrow: thither will I invite the Duke and all's contented followers. Go you and prepare Aliena; for look you, here comes my Rosalind.

ROSALIND   God save you, brother.

OLIVER   And you, fair sister.   [*Exit*

ROSALIND   O my dear Orlando, how it grieves me to see thee wear thy heart in a scarf!   20

ORLANDO   It is my arm.

ROSALIND   I thought thy heart had been wounded with the claws of a lion.

ORLANDO   Wounded it is, but with the eyes of a lady.

ROSALIND   Did your brother tell you how I counterfeited to sound when he showed me your handkercher?

ORLANDO   Ay, and greater wonders than that.

ROSALIND   O, I know where you are! Nay, 'tis true. There was never anything so sudden but the fight of 30 two rams and Caesar's thrasonical brag of 'I came, saw, and overcame'; for your brother and my sister no sooner met but they looked; no sooner looked but

[37] degrees   *a pun on the meanings 'stages' and 'flight of stairs'*

[38–9] incontinent   *a pun on the meanings 'hastily' and 'without chastity'*

[45–8] By so much . . . wishes for   *i.e. The extent of my sorrow will tomorrow be increased in exact proportion to my estimate of Oliver's happiness in fulfilling his wishes*

[53–69] Know of me then . . . danger   *Rosalind's style changes in this speech, becoming more business-like and more formal as she decides that the time for games of pretence is now over.*

[53] Know of me   *Learn from me*

[55] conceit   *intelligence, understanding*

[56] insomuch   *in as much as*

[58] draw   *win*

[59] grace me   *enhance my reputation*

[61] conversed   *associated*

[63] not damnable   *not incurring damnation (i.e. not practising black magic, which involved dealings with the devil)*

[64] gesture   *behaviour*

[66] straits   *circumstances*

[67] inconvenient   *unsuitable*

[68–9] human as she is   *i.e. in her true flesh, not as a mere spirit raised by magic*

[70] in sober meanings   *the plain truth (i.e. You're not joking, are you?)*

they loved; no sooner loved but they sighed; no
sooner sighed but they asked one another the reason;
no sooner knew the reason but they sought the
remedy: and in these degrees have they made a pair
of stairs to marriage, which they will climb incontinent, or else be incontinent before marriage. They
are in the very wrath of love, and they will together; 40
clubs cannot part them.

ORLANDO   They shall be married tomorrow, and I
will bid the Duke to the nuptial. But, O, how bitter
a thing it is to look into happiness through another
man's eyes! By so much the more shall I tomorrow
be at the height of heart-heaviness, by how much I
shall think my brother happy in having what he
wishes for.

ROSALIND   Why then, tomorrow I cannot serve your
turn for Rosalind?   50

ORLANDO   I can live no longer by thinking.

ROSALIND   I will weary you then no longer with idle
talking. Know of me then, for now I speak to some
purpose, that I know you are a gentleman of good
conceit. I speak not this that you should bear a good
opinion of my knowledge, insomuch I say I know
you are; neither do I labour for a greater esteem
than may in some little measure draw a belief from
you, to do yourself good, and not to grace me.
Believe then, if you please, that I can do strange 60
things. I have, since I was three year old, conversed
with a magician, most profound in his art and yet
not damnable. If you do love Rosalind so near the
heart as your gesture cries it out, when your brother
marries Aliena shall you marry her. I know into
what straits of fortune she is driven, and it is not
impossible to me, if it appear not inconvenient to you,
to set her before your eyes tomorrow, human as she
is, and without any danger.

ORLANDO   Speakest thou in sober meanings?   70

[71] tender *value*

[73] bid *summon*

[77] ungentleness *impoliteness, rough usage*

[79] study *aim*
[80] despiteful *contemptuous*

[83] Good shepherd . . . love *It is an irony, deliberately sustained by Rosalind in the rest of the scene, that she is thought to be unacquainted with love.*

[88] And I . . . no woman *Here Rosalind develops the irony, for (as the audience alone knows) this apparent denial of love is a hidden confession of it.*

[94] fantasy *uncontrolled imagination*

[98] trial *willingness to endure suffering*
     observance *humble respect*

ROSALIND By my life I do, which I tender dearly, though I say I am a magician. Therefore put you in your best array, bid your friends; for if you will be married tomorrow, you shall; and to Rosalind, if you will.

Enter SILVIUS *and* PHEBE

Look, here comes a lover of mine and a lover of hers.

PHEBE Youth, you have done me much ungentleness To show the letter that I writ to you.

ROSALIND I care not if I have. It is my study
     To seem despiteful and ungentle to you.   80
     You are there followed by a faithful shepherd:
     Look upon him, love him; he worships you.

PHEBE Good shepherd, tell this youth what 'tis to love.

SILVIUS It is to be all made of sighs and tears;
     And so am I for Phebe.

PHEBE And I for Ganymede.

ORLANDO And I for Rosalind.

ROSALIND And I for no woman.

SILVIUS It is to be all made of faith and service;
     And so am I for Phebe.   90

PHEBE And I for Ganymede.

ORLANDO And I for Rosalind.

ROSALIND And I for no woman.

SILVIUS It is to be all made of fantasy,
     All made of passion, and all made of wishes,
     All adoration, duty, and observance,
     All humbleness, all patience, and impatience,
     All purity, all trial, all observance;
     And so am I for Phebe.

PHEBE And so am I for Ganymede.   100

ORLANDO And so am I for Rosalind.

ROSALIND And so am I for no woman.

PHEBE [*To* ROSALIND] If this be so, why blame you me to love you?

[104] If this be so . . . love you? *Orlando's repetition of this line startles Rosalind into a surprised question. There is, however, no need to suppose that he has seen through her disguise, which by convention is impenetrable. Either his explanation in the next line is sincere, or the new prospect of reunion with Rosalind encourages him for a moment to a playful resumption of pretence. It is nevertheless enough to make Rosalind put a stop to the protestations.*

[108] howling . . . wolves *a comment on the monotony of the lovers' repeated lamentations*

[116] if what pleases . . . you *another 'despiteful' hit at Phebe. Rosalind suggests that married life with Phebe may not live up to Silvius's romantic vision of it.*

ACT FIVE, scene 3
Another brief linking scene, this time separating the promise of meeting from the reunion itself, is again marked by a song, different from the previous ones in its fitting emphasis on youth and spring rather than experience and winter. It is wholly appropriate to this stage of the play, when the forces of love approach their culmination.

[1] Tomorrow . . . day *Rosalind's repeated references to 'tomorrow' in the previous scene are now echoed by Touchstone, giving further promise of the coming ceremony of marriage.*
[4] dishonest *immodest*
[4-5] woman of the world *a married woman*
[10] for you *ready to meet your wishes*

SILVIUS [*To* PHEBE]   If this be so, why blame you me
     to love you?
ORLANDO   If this be so, why blame you me to love
     you?
ROSALIND   Why do you speak too, 'Why blame you
     me to love you?'
ORLANDO   To her that is not here, nor doth not hear.
ROSALIND   Pray you, no more of this; 'tis like the howl-
     ing of Irish wolves against the moon. [*To* SILVIUS]
     I will help you if I can. [*To* PHEBE] I would love   110
     you if I could. Tomorrow meet me all together.
     [*To* PHEBE] I will marry you if ever I marry woman,
     and I'll be married tomorrow. [*To* ORLANDO] I will
     satisfy you, if ever I satisfied man, and you shall be
     married tomorrow. [*To* SILVIUS] I will content you,
     if what pleases you contents you, and you shall be
     married tomorrow. [*To* ORLANDO] As you love
     Rosalind, meet. [*To* SILVIUS] As you love Phebe,
     meet. And as I love no woman, I'll meet. So fare
     you well. I have left you commands.   120
SILVIUS   I'll not fail, if I live.
PHEBE   Nor I.
ORLANDO   Nor I.   [*Exeunt*

Scene 3. *Enter* TOUCHSTONE *and* AUDREY

TOUCHSTONE   Tomorrow is the joyful day, Audrey;
     tomorrow will we be married.
AUDREY   I do desire it with all my heart; and I hope it
     is no dishonest desire to desire to be a woman of
     the world. Here come two of the banished Duke's
     pages.

                    Enter two PAGES

FIRST PAGE   Well met, honest gentleman.
TOUCHSTONE   By my troth, well met. Come, sit, sit,
     and a song!
SECOND PAGE   We are for you. Sit i'th'middle.   10

[11] clap . . . roundly *start it briskly without unnecessary delay*
[12] hawking *clearing the throat*
[13] the only prologues *merely the prologues*
[14] in a tune *in unison*

[16–39] It was a lover . . . the spring *This lovely song celebrates much of what has been won from the action of the play: the accomplishment of successful love, the fertility of spring following the rigours of winter, the vindication of youthful optimism, and life set in a pastoral landscape which is real and not idealised, yet full of freshness and beauty.*

[19] ringtime *time for exchanging rings at marriage*

[28] carol *song for a festival*

[36] prime *(i) perfection; (ii) spring*

[41] ditty *words*
[41–2] the note . . . untuneable *the music was very untuneful. Compare Touchstone's reactions to music with those of Jaques.*
[43] kept time *kept proper time in our singing*

FIRST PAGE Shall we clap into't roundly, without hawking or spitting or saying we are hoarse, which are the only prologues to a bad voice?

SECOND PAGE I'faith, i'faith! And both in a tune, like two gypsies on a horse.

PAGES [*Sing*]

It was a lover and his lass
   With a hey, and a ho, and a hey nonino,
That o'er the green cornfield did pass
   In springtime, the only pretty ringtime,
When birds do sing, hey ding a ding, ding.   20
Sweet lovers love the spring.

Between the acres of the rye,
   With a hey, and a ho, and a hey nonino,
These pretty country folks would lie
   In springtime, the only pretty ringtime,
When birds do sing, hey ding a ding, ding.
Sweet lovers love the spring.

This carol they began that hour,
   With a hey, and a ho, and a hey nonino,
How that a life was but a flower   30
   In springtime, the only pretty ringtime,
When birds do sing, hey ding a ding, ding.
Sweet lovers love the spring.

And therefore take the present time,
   With a hey, and a ho, and a hey nonino,
For love is crownèd with the prime
   In springtime, the only pretty ringtime,
When birds do sing, hey ding a ding, ding.
Sweet lovers love the spring.

TOUCHSTONE Truly, young gentlemen, though there   40
was no great matter in the ditty, yet the note was
very untuneable.

FIRST PAGE You are deceived, sir. We kept time, we lost not our time.

[45] **time lost** *a waste of time. Touchstone plays on 'lost not our time'.*

[47] **mend** *improve*

ACT FIVE, scene 4

So we come to the play's ending, with the successful outcome of Rosalind's long-sustained contrivances in the appearance of Hymen and the set of marriages, and the arrival of Jaques de Boys with his tale of Duke Frederick's (somewhat improbable) conversion. In these two events all the remaining romantic and political dissatisfactions are resolved in a completely happy conclusion.

[4] **fear they hope . . . fear** *fear they are only hoping against hope, but realise that in fact they are afraid*

[5] **compact is urged** *agreement is clarified*

TOUCHSTONE   By my troth, yes; I count it but time lost
to hear such a foolish song. God buy you, and God
mend your voices! Come, Audrey.   [*Exeunt*

:ene 4. *Enter* DUKE SENIOR, AMIENS, JAQUES, ORLANDO,
OLIVER *and* CELIA

DUKE SENIOR   Dost thou believe, Orlando, that the boy
Can do all this that he hath promised?
ORLANDO   I sometimes do believe, and sometimes do
not,
As those that fear they hope, and know they
fear.

Enter ROSALIND, SILVIUS *and* PHEBE

ROSALIND   Patience once more, whiles our compact is
urged.
[*To the* DUKE] You say, if I bring in your
Rosalind,
You will bestow her on Orlando here?
DUKE SENIOR   That would I, had I kingdoms to give
with her.
ROSALIND [*To* ORLANDO]   And you say you will have
her when I bring her?
ORLANDO   That would I, were I of all kingdoms king.   10
ROSALIND [*To* PHEBE]   You say you'll marry me, if I
be willing?
PHEBE   That will I, should I die the hour after.
ROSALIND   But if you do refuse to marry me,
You'll give yourself to this most faithful
shepherd?
PHEBE   So is the bargain.
ROSALIND [*To* SILVIUS]   You say that you'll have Phebe,
if she will?
SILVIUS   Though to have her and death were both one
thing.

[18] make . . . even *smooth all these matters out*

[27] lively *lifelike*
    favour *appearance*

[32] desperate *dangerous*

[34] Obscurèd *Hidden; and protected as by his magic 'circle'*

[35] toward *coming*

[41] motley-minded *having the mind as well as the apparel of a fool*

[44] purgation *trial*
    trod a measure *danced a stately dance*

[45] politic *devious*

[46] undone *ruined (by not paying for his clothes)*

[47] like to have fought *nearly fought. This is the beginning of Touchstone's prolonged mockery in this scene of the elaborate devices used by courtiers to evade any serious consequences of quarrelling.*

[48] ta'en up *made up, reconciled*

ROSALIND I have promised to make all this matter
    even.
    Keep you your word, O Duke, to give your
      daughter;
    You yours, Orlando, to receive his daughter;   20
    Keep you your word, Phebe, that you'll marry
      me,
    Or else, refusing me, to wed this shepherd;
    Keep your word, Silvius, that you'll marry her
    If she refuse me; and from hence I go,
    To make these doubts all even.

              [*Exit* ROSALIND *and* CELIA

DUKE SENIOR I do remember in this shepherd boy
    Some lively touches of my daughter's favour.

ORLANDO My lord, the first time that I ever saw him
    Methought he was a brother to your daughter.
    But, my good lord, this boy is forest-born,   30
    And hath been tutored in the rudiments
    Of many desperate studies by his uncle,
    Whom he reports to be a great magician,
    Obscured in the circle of this forest.

Enter TOUCHSTONE *and* AUDREY

JAQUES There is, sure, another flood toward, and
these couples are coming to the ark. Here comes a
pair of very strange beasts, which in all tongues are
called fools.

TOUCHSTONE Salutation and greeting to you all!

JAQUES Good my lord, bid him welcome. This is the   40
motley-minded gentleman that I have so often met
in the forest. He hath been a courtier, he swears.

TOUCHSTONE If any man doubt that, let him put me to
my purgation. I have trod a measure, I have flattered
a lady, I have been politic with my friend, smooth
with mine enemy, I have undone three tailors; I
have had four quarrels, and like to have fought one.

JAQUES And how was that ta'en up?

[51-2] Good my lord . . . fellow *Jaques' anxiety for Touchstone to win approval is another sign of the curious attraction they have for each other – similar men in some respects, opposite in others.*

[54] God 'ield you *God reward you*

[54-5] I desire . . . like *either 'May I return the compliment?' or 'I hope you will go on doing so'*

[56] copulatives *those about to be married (but the word has, of course, Touchstone's characteristic reductive anti-romanticism)*

[57] blood breaks *passion cools*

[58] ill-favoured *ugly*

[59] humour *whim. (Is Touchstone lying? If so, why?)*

[60] honesty *chastity*

[62] swift and sententious *quick-witted and wise*

[64] fool's bolt *derived from the proverb 'a fool's bolt is soon shot'*

[65] dulcet diseases *probably 'pleasant shortcomings', such as being unable to refrain from a fool's 'flouting'*

[66] But for *But, with regard to*

[69] seeming *becomingly*

[70] dislike *express dislike of*

[72] in the mind *of the opinion that*

[75] Quip *Retort*
   If again *If I said again*

[76] disabled *belittled*

[81] Circumstantial *Indirect, depending on the circumstances*

TOUCHSTONE Faith, we met, and found the quarrel was upon the seventh cause. 50

JAQUES How seventh cause? Good my lord, like this fellow.

DUKE SENIOR I like him very well.

TOUCHSTONE God 'ield you, sir; I desire you of the like. I press in here, sir, amongst the rest of the country copulatives, to swear and to forswear, according as marriage binds and blood breaks. A poor virgin, sir, an ill-favoured thing, sir, but mine own; a poor humour of mine, sir, to take that that no man else will. Rich honesty dwells like a miser, sir, 60 in a poor house, as your pearl in your foul oyster.

DUKE SENIOR By my faith, he is very swift and sententious.

TOUCHSTONE According to the fool's bolt, sir, and such dulcet diseases.

JAQUES But for the seventh cause. How did you find the quarrel on the seventh cause?

TOUCHSTONE Upon a lie seven times removed. Bear your body more seeming, Audrey. As thus, sir. I did dislike the cut of a certain courtier's beard. He 70 sent me word, if I said his beard was not cut well, he was in the mind it was: this is called the Retort Courteous. If I sent him word again it was not well cut, he would send me word he cut it to please himself: this is called the Quip Modest. If again, 'it was not well cut,' he disabled my judgement: this is called the Reply Churlish. If again, 'it was not well cut', he would answer, I spake not true: this is called the Reproof Valiant. If again, 'it was not well cut,' he would say I lie: this is called the Countercheck 80 Quarrelsome: and so to the Lie Circumstantial and the Lie Direct.

JAQUES And how oft did you say his beard was not well cut?

TOUCHSTONE I durst go no further than the Lie

[87] measured   *to make sure, prior to a duel, that the swords were of equal length (in this case a pure formality)*

[90] in print   *according to the book of rules*

[99] take up   *make up*
[100–1] thought but of   *merely thought of*

[102] swore brothers   *swore to behave like brothers*

[106] stalking-horse   *a horse behind which the hunter takes cover when stalking game*
[107] presentation   *appearance (deceptive, of course, in that Touchstone's folly is assumed)*

Enter HYMEN   *Hymen may be played by one of the other characters, briefed for the part by Rosalind. The singer Amiens has been suggested as one possibility. Or it may be regarded as a real intervention by magic of the goddess of marriage. Each director has to decide about this, but the over-all effect of the occasion is not as a rule greatly affected.*

[109] made even   *smoothed out*
[110] Atone together   *Are reconciled*

Circumstantial, nor he durst not give me the Lie
Direct. And so we measured swords and parted.

JAQUES Can you nominate in order now the degrees
of the lie?

TOUCHSTONE O sir, we quarrel in print, by the book, 90
as you have books for good manners. I will name
you the degrees. The first, the Retort Courteous;
the second, the Quip Modest; the third, the Reply
Churlish; the fourth, the Reproof Valiant; the fifth,
the Countercheck Quarrelsome; the sixth, the Lie
with Circumstance; the seventh, the Lie Direct.
All these you may avoid but the Lie Direct, and you
may avoid that too, with an 'If'. I knew when seven
justices could not take up a quarrel, but when the
parties were met themselves, one of them thought 100
but of an 'If': as, 'If you said so, then I said so';
and they shook hands and swore brothers. Your 'If'
is the only peacemaker. Much virtue in 'If'.

JAQUES Is not this a rare fellow, my lord? He's as good
at anything, and yet a fool.

DUKE SENIOR He uses his folly like a stalking horse,
and under the presentation of that he shoots his wit.

Enter HYMEN, *followed by* ROSALIND *and* CELIA,
no longer disguised. Soft music.

HYMEN   Then is there mirth in heaven
           When earthly things made even
               Atone together.   110
           Good Duke, receive thy daughter;
           Hymen from heaven brought her,
               Yea, brought her hither,
           That thou mightst join her hand with his
           Whose heart within her bosom is.

ROSALIND [*To* DUKE] To you I give myself, for I am
    yours.
    [*To* ORLANDO] To you I give myself, for I am yours.

191

[125] bar *forbid*

[129] Hymen's bands *the bands or bond of marriage*
[130] holds true contents *is to remain true to its word*

[131] cross *affliction*

[133] accord *consent*

[135] sure together *bound up together*

[139] reason ... diminish *explanation may reduce your astonish-*
ment

DUKE SENIOR If there be truth in sight, you are my
    daughter.

ORLANDO If there be truth in sight, you are my
    Rosalind.

PHEBE If sight and shape be true,   120
    Why then, my love adieu!

ROSALIND [*To* DUKE] I'll have no father, if you be not
    he.

  [*To* ORLANDO] I'll have no husband, if you be not
    he.

  [*To* PHEBE] Nor ne'er wed woman, if you be not
    she.

HYMEN Peace ho! I bar confusion:
    'Tis I must make conclusion
    Of these most strange events.
    Here's eight that must take hands
    To join in Hymen's bands,
    If truth holds true contents.   130
    [*To* ORLANDO *and* ROSALIND]
    You and you no cross shall part.
    [*To* OLIVER *and* CELIA]
    You and you are heart in heart.
    [*To* PHEBE]
    You to his love must accord,
    Or have a woman to your lord.
    [*To* TOUCHSTONE *and* AUDREY]
    You and you are sure together
    As the winter to foul weather.
    [*To all*]
    Whiles a wedlock hymn we sing,
    Feed yourselves with questioning,
    That reason wonder may diminish
    How thus we met, and these things finish.   140

SONG
Wedding is great Juno's crown,
  O blessèd bond of board and bed!

[144] High *Highly*

[148] Even daughter *Either (to Celia) 'as much as if you were my daughter' or (to Rosalind) 'and also you, my true daughter'*

[150] Thy faith . . . combine *Your faithfulness binds my love to you*

[156] Addressed *Made ready*
      power *army*
[157] In . . . conduct *Under his own leadership*

[159] skirts *fringe*
[160] religious man *man dedicated to some service of religion (possibly a hermit)*
[161] question *talk*
[162] the world *the society of men*

[166] engage *pledge*

[167] offer'st fairly *bring a handsome gift*
[168] one . . . other *(i) Oliver and (ii) Orlando (who will inherit the dukedom by his marriage to Rosalind)*
[169] at large *in absolute possession*
[170] do those ends *perform those aims*
[172] every *every one*
[173] shrewd *(i) grievous; (ii) sharp with cold*

'Tis Hymen peoples every town;
　High wedlock then be honourèd.
Honour, high honour, and renown
　To Hymen, god of every town!

DUKE SENIOR　O my dear niece, welcome thou art to me,
　Even daughter, welcome, in no less degree!

PHEBE [*To* SILVIUS]　I will not eat my word, now thou
　art mine;
　Thy faith my fancy to thee doth combine.　　　150

Enter Second Brother, JAQUES DE BOYS

SECOND BROTHER　Let me have audience for a word or
　two.
　I am the second son of old Sir Rowland
　That bring these tidings to this fair assembly.
　Duke Frederick, hearing how that every day
　Men of great worth resorted to this forest,
　Addressed a mighty power, which were on foot
　In his own conduct, purposely to take
　His brother here and put him to the sword;
　And to the skirts of this wild wood he came,
　Where, meeting with an old religious man,　　　160
　After some question with him, was converted
　Both from his enterprise, and from the world,
　His crown bequeathing to his banished brother,
　And all their lands restored to them again
　That were with him exiled. This to be true
　I do engage my life.

DUKE SENIOR　　　　　　　　Welcome, young man.
　Thou offer'st fairly to thy brothers' wedding:
　To one, his lands withheld; and to the other,
　A land itself at large, a potent dukedom.
　First, in this forest let us do those ends　　　170
　That here were well begun and well begot;
　And after, every of this happy number
　That have endured shrewd days and nights with
　　us

[175] According ... states   *In proportion to their rank*

[179] With measure   *In good measure*
measures   *stately dances. The Duke plays on various meanings of 'measure'.*
[180] Sir, ... patience   *Jaques apologises to the Duke for interrupting before addressing Jaques de Boys.*
[182] thrown into neglect   *renounced his interest in*
pompous   *full of pomp*
[184] convertites   *religious converts*

[192] Is ... victualled   *Carries supplies for no more than two months*

[195] would have   *wish to ask*

[201-2] good wine ... bush   *a proverb, based on the vintner's custom of hanging a 'bush' outside his shop. It means 'Good things need no advertisement'.*

Shall share the good of our returned fortune,
According to the measure of their states.
Meantime forget this new-fall'n dignity
And fall into our rustic revelry.
Play, music, and you brides and bridegrooms
    all,
With measure heaped in joy, to th'measures fall.

JAQUES   Sir, by your patience. If I heard you rightly,   180
The Duke hath put on a religious life
And thrown into neglect the pompous court.

SECOND BROTHER   He hath.

JAQUES   To him will I. Out of these convertites
There is much matter to be heard and learned.
[*To* DUKE]   You to your former honour I
    bequeath;
Your patience and your virtue well deserves it.
[*To* ORLANDO]   You to a love that your true
    faith doth merit;
[*To* OLIVER]   You to your land and love and
    great allies;
[*To* SILVIUS]   You to a long and well-deservèd
    bed;   190
[*To* TOUCHSTONE]   And you to wrangling, for
    thy loving voyage
Is but for two months victualled. So, to your
    pleasures:
I am for other than for dancing measures.

DUKE SENIOR   Stay, Jaques, stay.

JAQUES   To see no pastime, I. What you would have
I'll stay to know at your abandoned cave.   [*Exit*

DUKE SENIOR   Proceed, proceed. We will begin these
    rites,
As we do trust they'll end, in true delights.
       [*Exeunt, after the dance, all except* ROSALIND

ROSALIND   It is not the fashion to see the lady the
epilogue, but it is no more unhandsome than to see 200
the lord the prologue. If it be true that good wine

[205] case   *(i) situation; (ii) costume*
[206] insinuate with you   *win your approval*
[207] furnished   *dressed*

[209] conjure you   *cast a spell on you (a continuation from
Rosalind's recent pretence of magicianship)*

[215] If I were a woman   *Rosalind, along with all other femal
roles, was originally played by a boy.*
[217] liked   *pleased*
       defied not   *was not offended by*

[220] bid me farewell   *i.e. applaud*

needs no bush, 'tis true that a good play needs no epilogue. Yet to good wine they do use good bushes, and good plays prove the better by the help of good epilogues. What a case am I in then, that am neither a good epilogue, nor cannot insinuate with you in the behalf of a good play! I am not furnished like a beggar; therefore to beg will not become me. My way is to conjure you, and I'll begin with the women. I charge you, O women, for the love you bear to men, 210 to like as much of this play as please you; and I charge you, O men, for the love you bear to women — as I perceive by your simpering, none of you hates them — that between you and the women the play may please. If I were a woman, I would kiss as many of you as had beards that pleased me, complexions that liked me, and breaths that I defied not; and I am sure, as many as have good beards, or good faces, or sweet breaths, will, for my kind offer, when I make curtsy, bid me farewell. [*Exit* 220